Almost Aviation
Building beautiful flight simulator control panels

by
Mark Hurst

Almost Aviation
By Mark Hurst

www.almostaviation.com

Foreword

Aviation may not be in my blood, but it's always been in my bedroom. As long as I can remember I have been fascinated by anything to do with aircraft and aviation. I built Airfix kits and balsa models, demanded aeroplane toys and games for Christmas and once scratch-built a working ornithopter model from plans I found in the *Children's Britannica*. My first real flying was in open-cockpit air cadet gliders and after that I dabbled (briefly) in hang-gliding and made a handful of parachute jumps. In 1993 I went to California for a month and scored a PPL, but while I kept it up for a few years my forays into aviation were sporadic and my licence lapsed with around 100 hours in my log book.

But the fascination remained. The home computer revolution was just starting as I left school and an interest in flight simulation was inevitable. Unlike the real thing, flight simulation is amenable to dabbling, and so dabble I did for a couple of decades until the technology began to catch up. I ran *Nite Flite* on the ZX Spectrum, *Aviator* on the BBC Micro at work and Sublogic's *Flight Simulator II* on the Atari ST. I spent a fortune on rickety hardware like the MAXX and Zoomer yokes, was an early adopter of such innovations as the original 'yoghurt carton and bath-plug chain' rudder pedals from CH Products and later of more credible efforts like the CH Virtual Pilot yoke and the Thrustmaster RCS pedals.

In time, the technology moved on and in 2009 I started experimenting with Microsoft Flight Simulator X using increasingly realistic simulator setups. I tried many solutions for the buttons and switches you need to fly an aircraft without the mouse and keyboard but ultimately I was frustrated because the panels I could buy from the likes of Saitek and VR Insight always seemed too generic or too limited – they never had enough buttons or switches, and the buttons and switches they did have never seemed to be the right ones for what I needed.

It was Aerosoft's Twin Otter Extended that changed things for me. Here was a detailed simulation and I was excited by the idea of building some kind of enclosed cockpit for it. Having recently acquired a VR Insight switch panel, my original notion was that I'd just buy a few more of these and cluster them around me to give the feeling of sitting in a real cockpit. When I counted up the number of switches I would need I realised this wasn't a good idea. The Twin Otter Extended needs 179 switches for a near-complete implementation and I soon saw that if I was to get anything approaching a realistic layout I would need to build the panels myself.

And why not? These days it is very easy to interface switches to FSX with off-the-shelf joystick controllers and software such as FSUIPC, and this is what I decided to do. You can follow the genesis of the Twin Otter cockpit on my YouTube channel (Almost Aviation) but it was the experience of building the Twin Otter that led to the simplified panels I will describe here.

I am happy to report that having a handful of custom panels that do exactly what I need them to do has transformed my experience of flying aircraft in FSX. Not only that, but the building of a working panel turned out to be almost as straightforward as it appeared at the outset. I am confident that doing the same is well within the capabilities of anyone with a moderately technical eye and a measure of patience. (Which surely describes anyone who has spent a bit of time with FSX!)

I hope you will join me in building your own panels. You can visit the forum at www.almostaviation.com to discuss the ins and outs of anything you read here with like-minded builders and I will do my best to answer any questions you may have about building. You can download the graphics templates and updates of the Almost Aviation library and if you want a quick-start build you will also be able to purchase pre-manufactured acrylic panels for the GPS and autopilot. There may be further kit-build options in the future.

The view from the Twin Otter

Table of contents

Introduction

This guide will show you how to build fully-functional
hardware panels to drive the autopilot and/or GPS in your
Microsoft Flight Simulator X aircraft. You can build your
panels from scratch, without any specialist knowledge, and the
result will be of a quality that is close to a real aircraft panel. I
have designed two specific panels – one for the autopilot and
one for the GPS – but you could use the techniques described
here to build a custom panel of your own design.

You can build the panels described here using common DIY tools. At a minimum you will need a power drill and hacksaw blades for creating the acrylic panels and a soldering iron for doing the wiring. The panel graphics can be printed on a regular desktop inkjet or laser printer. The raw materials for the physical panel construction are available at your local DIY store. The buttons and switches, of course, are more specialist items that you will likely need to order online. You will find a full suggested component list, including suppliers, in Appendix B.

The panels described here are based on a device that presents to Windows as a standard joystick controller. Although I have written this guide around the development of panels specifically for Microsoft Flight Simulator X (a.k.a. FSX) you will very likely be able to use the information here to create panels for other flight simulators too. Lockheed Martin's Prepare3D (a.k.a. P3D) interfaces to controllers in exactly the same way as FSX so everything written here will apply to P3D in all but the minor details.

The panels you build will interface to FSX in exactly the same way as commercially-available panels such as those from Saitek, VR Insight or GoFlight. This means they will be as easy to interface as those panels but also that they will have the same limitations. There is no magic here – you will be able to hook up your panels to standard FSX functions but interfacing to non-standard add-on aircraft will take a little more work. However, you will be able to get your Autopilot and GPS panels working with many common add-on payware aircraft, often with minimal effort.

If you build either of the panels described here you can connect it up to FSX using any of the common methods, but I have described in detail how to do it using FSUIPC and LINDA. This is by far the simplest and most flexible way of connecting hardware to FSX but it does require that you purchase a licence for FSUIPC. My purpose is not to sell you FSUIPC but most consider it an essential for connecting FSX to buttons and switches and joysticks. FSUIPC is also a most impressive example of mature software. From my own experience, if there is something you want to do with buttons and switches in FSX, and if it makes logical sense, you can be confident that FSUIPC provides a way to do it.

I designed the panels here as a simplification of the GPS and autopilot panels I built for my Twin Otter home cockpit. The construction and interfacing methods described here are identical to that build but I have refined the panels to be more generic and less ambitious than my originals, to keep costs down but also to make a scratch-build more within reach of the casual hobbyist. If you are feeling more confident you could easily adapt what you find here to add a screen to your GPS, like the one in my Twin Otter cockpit.

Building the hardware

In summary, the construction goes like this. You will cut two identical rectangular panels from a 2mm clear acrylic sheet and sandwich them together, fastening them with two machine screws. I typically use 3mm or 4mm screws with a flat or pan head. These screws hold the panels together during construction and help keep the graphic insert registered. The panel graphics and captions are printed on a regular inkjet or laser printer and are sandwiched between the two acrylic panels. The result is a high-quality and professional-looking panel fascia.

The graphic insert can be printed on paper or on clear acetates. Depending on your choice of printing materials you can choose to make your panels backlit or not. During construction you will use a simpler schematic graphic that is marked with cross-hairs showing where to drill the holes. The panels are designed exclusively around components that mount through circular holes. The advantage is that circular holes are much easier to cut precisely with a power drill. Once all the holes are cut, the final graphic can be printed and the components mounted on the panel.

Once the components are in place you need to think about how you are going to mount the finished panels in your simpit. I built the panels for my Twin Otter cockpit as independent units, each mounted on a frame made from 25mm x 50mm (1" x 2") timber. Each panel is effectively a shallow box with one side (the rear) missing. An advantage of this method is that the components and wiring are well-protected from bumps and the panel is quite sturdy and robust. I also used connectors to make the wiring detachable so I could remove individual panels and tinker with them.

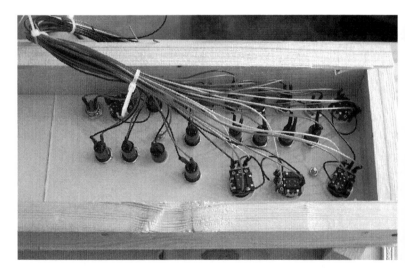

You may choose instead to mount your panels flush on a dash, which is arguably easier. It also allows you to customise the layout if you build more than one panel or have other hardware

to mount. 3mm MDF is a good choice of material for a dash –
it is cheap, very easy to work with and is sufficiently rigid as
long as you don't use large expanses without timber bracing.
Alternatively, if you are building a single panel you might
want to build some kind of box that can sit on your desktop
and mount it on that. The panels are designed with all the
components well clear of a 25mm margin all round, which
ensures flexibility of mounting and that all the graphics can be
back-lit.

Working on an MDF panel

For mounting the panels themselves, it is important to use
appropriate fixings or you risk cracking the acrylic. You can
use pan-headed or dome-headed screws, which have a flat
underside, but I have chosen to use counter-sunk screws with

5

cup washers. This applies the mechanical load away from the hole and also looks pretty good.

After physical construction of the panel you will need to wire up the components. All components are effectively simple push-to-make switches that connect directly to the inputs of the controller board. The rotary encoder switches are wired as three independent push-to-make switches (or five if you choose to use dual concentric encoders).

Creating the panel fascia

The panel fascia is made from 2mm clear acrylic sheeting. You can use other materials, although if you do that some of the instructions in the rest of this manual will be of limited use. For example, 3mm MDF (medium density fibreboard) is a good choice for easy construction or for building prototypes but it won't be possible to make backlit panels and you will need an alternative way to finish the surface and apply the graphics.

Acrylic (also known by brand names such as Perspex, Plexiglas and Lucite) is a hard but flexible clear plastic. It comes in various thicknesses and a typical use is for glazing of greenhouses and sheds. It is relatively cheap and is easily available from DIY outlets such as B&Q, Homebase and Wickes. For this application the 2mm sheets are most appropriate. At first sight this material seems too flexible to make a rigid panel, but you're going to build the panel by making a sandwich of two sheets, which in my experience is quite rigid enough for panels at least up to 30cm square.

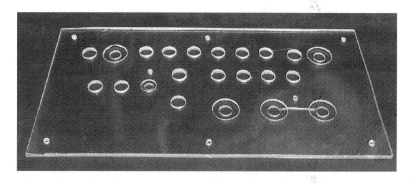

Your panels will measure 28cm x 15cm. This gives a chunky, rugged panel with good component spacing and it leaves plenty of room for graphics and captions while keeping realistic tolerances for hand-built construction. The acrylic sheets typically come in sizes that are multiples of 30cm (120cm x 60cm is the smallest size generally available from DIY stores) and while it requires fewer cuts to make a 30cm wide panel I would not recommend doing so. This is for the simple reason that most people will only have access to an A4 printer and hence won't be able to print the graphics for a 30cm panel on a single sheet. This is worse if you want to use clear film for the graphics as you will need to use more than one layer to get the required density.

Arguably, cutting and drilling the panel fascias from acrylic is the hardest part of this whole project. Acrylic can be cut and drilled but it is not an easy material to work with and there is great scope for catastrophe if you make a mistake. Acrylic is a very brittle material and is prone to cracking. It will also melt if you attempt to cut or drill it too quickly and while this isn't in itself catastrophic, melting and re-setting can cause subsequent shock-loading by the drill bit or saw and this in turn can lead to cracking.

WARNING: WEAR EYE PROTECTION WHEN CUTTING OR DRILLING ACRYLIC!

Following the guidelines below should maximise your chances of cutting and drilling acrylic sheets without problems. However, it is very important to wear eye protection because acrylic can chip and crack abruptly under mechanical load. This is particularly likely when drilling, when you may be hit by very sharp chips of acrylic ejected at high velocity. If you buy your acrylic sheets from a DIY store you will likely have more than you need, so I recommend practising your cutting and drilling techniques on scraps before starting the construction of your panel proper.

You will invariably find that acrylic sheeting comes with the surfaces protected by a self-adhesive film. In spite of this it is almost inevitable that the sheets found in a DIY store will be a bit road-weary after transit and storage so you want to make sure you select one with a minimum of scratching. Remember that you will be making a sandwich of two sheets and while scratches on the rearmost sheet are inconsequential you want the front sheet to be as close to unblemished as possible.

I purchased my acrylic sheets from Homebase under the brand 'Liteglaze' and with this brand you will find that one side of the sheet has a near-opaque film cover and the other has a clear film with text and branding printed on it. You should attend to these differences carefully during construction because you will need to remove the opaque film from the underside of the uppermost sheet of your sandwich so that you can see the graphics showing where to drill the holes. If you accidentally remove the film from the wrong side you will end up working at some length with an unprotected surface, making it very likely that your finished panel will have at least a few scratches on it.

Cutting the acrylic sheets

There are a few ways of cutting acrylic. If you buy the Liteglaze brand you will find some tips printed on the clear protective film. This is annoying as it will get in the way of your hole-drilling guide graphics during construction, but it also suggests the score-and-snap method, which I don't recommend for this application. Firstly, scoring the surface can itself be quite hazardous, particularly if you use something like a sharp craft (Stanley) knife. The nature of acrylic means it becomes tacky and melts under high pressure and if you are too casual with your work it is easy to get into a situation where the knife binds and leads to unpredictable and dangerous jerky movements. If you do intend to use this method it is safer to use a glass-scoring tool. However, even the best score-and-snap cut will give you rough edges and likely some chipping at the ends. This means you will need to tidy up the edges and that your top and bottom sheets are unlikely to be exactly the same size.

I have found the most effective way to cut an acrylic sheet is with a hacksaw. A traditional hacksaw (where the blade forms the long side of a large D shape) is unlikely to be able to make a 28cm cut so you will need to find an alternative. A fine-toothed hand-saw with an unsupported blade is ideal, but if you don't have one you ought to be able to make one by improvising your own handle for an unsupported hacksaw blade. It's then a matter of marking the acrylic with an indelible felt-tipped pen and cutting a straight line.

An unsupported hand saw with interchangeable blades

For making the cut it is important to clamp the acrylic sheet securely. Take care to protect all surfaces by clamping against something soft like blocks of wood or hardboard and to clear shaving and debris when re-positioning and re-clamping. It is also very important to support the free end of the acrylic sheet, especially when initially working with larger pieces. Any loose end will try its best to flap up and down with the action of the saw and this can lead to catastrophic cracking of the whole sheet. You need to think in two dimensions when considering support. An unsupported end outboard of the cut will flap up and down parallel with the cut, but as the cut progresses, the increasingly unsupported waste piece will flap up and down perpendicularly, leading to additional shearing forces at the site of the cut. The best advice is to clamp and re-clamp everything as many times as you need to in order to complete a cut without anything flapping at all. If everything is well-clamped the material saws very easily and produces a fine cut with powdery acrylic sawdust. As with all sawing – but crucially with acrylic – it is important to keep the saw moving because abrupt stick/un-sticking events lead to those mechanical torquing forces that provoke cracking.

To ensure a straight cut I have experimented with clamping guides along the edge of my cut – for example, wooden battens and metal rulers, whether on one side or both sides (i.e. left and right) of the cut. However, often simpler is better and I have achieved excellent results simply by following the line of the pen mark by hand and taking it slowly, steering the saw back on track if it begins to depart. I have not found melting to be a problem with hand-sawing, although undoubtedly it will be if you saw too vigorously. I have read that you can use a jigsaw but I have not tried this.

Even with unguided hand-sawing as described I have achieved very clean cuts of a quality that is acceptable without any finishing. I have also found that even cutting the two (upper and lower) sheets independently the results can be close enough in size. This is in stark contrast to my Twin Otter panels, which were created with the score-and-snap method and which do not stand up well under too-close scrutiny. You may, of course, choose to clamp two pieces of acrylic together and cut them both at the same time. I have not tried this extensively so I suggest you experiment with scrap material before doing this for real. I did cut a hole this way for the screen in my Twin Otter GPS panel, but that was quite a rough cut because I knew it was going to be hidden behind the monitor bezel.

Incidentally, to cut a hole out of an acrylic sheet with a saw you will need to make an initial hole to insert the saw. If you want to do this I suggest you make the hole significantly inside the waste area because it's going to be quite ugly and a bit unpredictable. I try to drill a number of holes close together with a small drill bit (e.g. 2mm) and then try to connect them up by drilling obliquely into the walls of the holes. Once you have a slot big enough to insert the saw, you can then carefully begin cutting and steering the cut out towards the edge of the area you have marked for cutting. Don't try to do this too assertively, just accept that you will need to tidy up part of your eventual cut-out with a file.

If any finishing or adjustment of the edges is required, it can be done safely with a fine-toothed file and/or sandpaper. I do recommend that you use a file to add a slight radius to the corners, which are otherwise quite sharp. You may want to add a slight bevel to the edges, although if you plan to do this it is wise to practise on a scrap sheet because it is not easy to get it uniform along an edge. Take care if using sandpaper once you have removed the protective film from your front panel as it is easy to accidentally scratch the surface.

Mounting the components

Once you have our panels cut to size, the next step is to drill the holes for mounting the components. Before getting into the specifics of making the holes let's just take a look at what you're aiming to do. The panels have been designed so that all the components are mounted in circular holes, although these holes are not all of the same size. Components mount in two ways – either the component is inserted from the front and secured by a nut at the rear of the panel, or the other way around.

On the two specific panels I have designed (GPS and Autopilot), the push-buttons are secured with a nut at the rear and the rotary controls by a nut at the front. The push-buttons also include optional spring washers, which I tend not to use because they are visible and detract from the final appearance. These are generally intended to keep the component tightly-seated under vibration, which ought in any case to make them unnecessary in a flight simulator cockpit, but you can use them behind the panel (under the nut) if you wish. The rotary controls have knurled washers to prevent them rotating in the socket when operated. I do recommend using these and as they are mounted behind the panel they will not be visible. The GPS panel includes one latching push-button that has a front-mounted nut.

The general plan is to secure the two acrylic panels together and then drill the holes through both sheets at once. The first step is to print a sheet with an actual-size graphic showing all the hole centres (see later) and then carefully centre this up between the two acrylic sheets before taping them together at all four edges. The next step is to drill the two registration holes and insert the screws to hold the two panels and the graphic together securely for the rest of the construction. (Don't do this until you have read the notes on drilling and types of drill bit below.) This is more reliable than the tape and it also guarantees more secure registration of the guide graphic during drilling and also of the final graphic during assembly.

So far, so good. Of course things are rarely so simple in practice and indeed you will discover a constraint in the panel thickness. While some of the components will mount easily on the two-panel (4+mm) sandwich, some of them will not because the panel is too thick. The rotary encoders, in particular, have a ¼" (6.35mm) threaded bushing which is, in practice, too short. For these components you need to cut a larger hole in the rear sheet than in the front sheet. This allows you to mount the component on the front sheet only (2mm thick), while the bigger hole in the rear sheet leaves enough space around the component so that it doesn't interfere. You will see that if you are going to substitute any components for the ones I have specified you will need to carefully research the bushing lengths (and, of course, the diameters) and adjust the specifics of the holes you drill to suit.

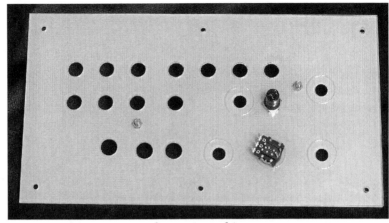

A rotary encoder mounted in a rear cut-out

An aside – creating the guide graphic

Before you are ready to drill the holes to mount the
components you need to know precisely where to drill them.
You could measure and mark directly on the panels, but a
simpler option is to produce a full-size graphic that you can
mount between the panels. You could use the final graphic
directly but you more than likely want to produce something
less cluttered with only the hole centres marked. Printing this
black on white rather than in whatever final colour scheme you
have chosen is obviously more economical.

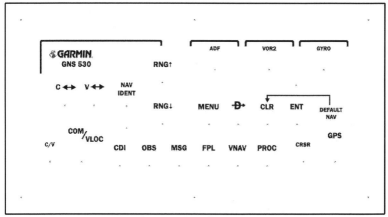

Guide graphic for the GPS

You will find all the information you need to create your panel graphics, whether the final version or the drilling guide, in appendix A.

Drilling the acrylic panels

Assuming you have the panels taped together with the guide graphic in place, it's now time to drill the holes. The main thing to be aware of when drilling a thin acrylic sheet is that you need to prevent any push-pull deformation of the surface because this will lead to cracking. As you will be bearing down in the work piece to cut a hole, it is essential to support it from underneath by a block of wood (often called a 'sacrificial back piece' as you'll drill into it when you break through the work piece). The next thing is to select an appropriate drill bit that will not apply any pulling force to the acrylic sheet. This means that regular helical twist bits (which may be black, grey or gold-coloured) are generally not appropriate as they can exert an upward pull on the material. This is especially true if you trying to enlarge an existing hole by using a slightly bigger bit, as this will inevitably grab the material and crack or even shatter it. Likewise, stay away from helical auger bits which are intended for drilling wood with a hand drill.

If you do need to enlarge a hole, you can get away with using a smaller bit and rolling it around in the hole while it's spinning. This is only really suitable for holes that are only slightly too small and you likely won't end up with a very round hole. A safer way to do it is to wrap some sandpaper around a pencil or a drill bit (depending on how big the existing hole is) and rub this around the inside of the hole in a circular motion. If you made a mistake and got the hole size way too small you're going to have to resort to using small needle files or something to gradually increase the size of the hole manually.

For smaller diameter holes (in my experience up to 4mm) you can get away with twist bits but it is wise to drill slowly. You will also find that drilling through a two-sheet sandwich requires additional care because as you break through the upper sheet it tends to be pushed upwards as the lower sheet resists the initial penetration. Again, keeping it slow is wise. You will soon learn to sense the change in sound and in the resistance of the drill as it approaches the breakthrough, so again it is useful to have a few practice goes on scrap material before diving in and experimenting on your carefully-cut panels.

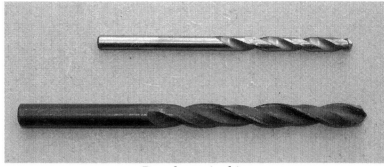

Regular twist bits

There are two types of drill that are safe to use on 2mm acrylic sheets. These are 'brad point' bits and 'spade' or 'paddle' bits. Both are intended for woodwork and both cut the hole with a circular downward-bearing action. The brad point is a helical bit with a centre point and two sharp spurs out at the edges. The centre point keeps the drill centred while the spurs cut the hole. The spade bit has a similar action but is flat, not helical. The range of sizes available for each of these two kinds if bit is different but overlapping; the largest brad point bit I could find was 12mm, while the spade bits go up to 30mm or more. There is a third type of bit that might work, although I haven't tried it. This is a 'hole saw', which is more like a cylindrical saw with a central helical bit to guide it. These look expensive and don't seem to come in many sizes, but you might be able to find what you need.

Brad-point bits

You will need to cut holes of the following sizes: 4mm, 7mm, 10mm, 12mm, 13mm and 22mm. You will also need a 1mm bit (1.5mm or 2mm would probably do) for drilling pilot holes. The total number of separate drilling operations you will need to complete without incident is 42 if you are building the GPS panel and/or 38 if you are building the Autopilot panel. (Although in each case, eight of these are simple 4mm holes and a further five or six are 1mm pilot holes for locating the cut-outs on the rear sheet for the shallow-mount components.)

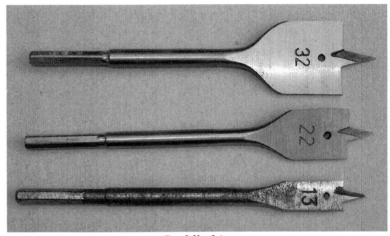

Paddle bits

Before drilling any holes it's a good idea to review the sizes and make sure you know what you're going to drill where. You can either include the sizes on your guide graphic or you can write them onto the acrylic (which has a film cover over it, remember) with a marker pen. You should also clearly mark the holes that require a bigger cut-out on the back sheet. For these holes it's vital not to drill the smaller hole all the way through first, because then it's going to be impossible to make the back hole bigger. I suggest you do things in the order I describe below.

WARNING: REMEMBER TO USE EYE PROTECTION! I MEAN IT!

First, drill the two 4mm holes for screwing the acrylic sheets together. Then, before doing anything else, insert the screws and tighten the nuts up. Tighten these a little past finger-tight but don't over-tighten with a spanner or, you guessed it, you'll crack the acrylic. I suggest you leave the tape on the edges too as this will help keep everything stable.

Now drill the rest of the 4mm holes, which are the six peripheral holes for mounting the finished panel. These are the easiest and you will get used to the routine of clamping and the feel of the drill. Clamp either side of the holes where possible, and beware of the corner holes where you can't do that because the upper sheet will want to lift as you break through it. Remember, take it slow.

Next, I suggest you drill the pilot holes for the components that require the two-hole tap dance. Use a 1mm drill if you have it, otherwise the smallest bit you have. Drill all the way through the two sheets, again clamping either side each time. A 1mm bit is very fragile so take care not so put any lateral forces on it or it may snap. Do not drill the full-sized holes yet. I suggest that once you have drilled these pilot holes (six on the GPS panel, five on the Autopilot panel) you then use a marker to mark them with a big cross or something to remind you to steer clear. You will only drill these holes later, after separating the two acrylic sheets.

Now it's time to drill the medium-sized holes. These are all either 12mm or 13mm in diameter. Again, make sure it's clear which size you're drilling. The 12mm holes are for the square push-buttons and the 13mm holes are for the round push-buttons. It isn't disastrous if you get one wrong – the square buttons will go in a 13mm hole but may not line up as easily; the round buttons will need a 12mm hole enlarged slightly before they will fit. If you do make this mistake, don't try to screw the round button into a 12mm hole – at best you will damage the button because you will doubtless end up using pliers or something, and at worst you will crack the acrylic.

Again, clamp the work piece on either side of the hole you're about to drill. If you have a choice of bits, use a brad point bit in preference to a spade bit. The brad point will cut a deep groove that will take you most of the way through the acrylic, while the spade will essentially scrape a tunnel through the acrylic at almost the full width of the hole. This takes more work and generates more heat. (And hence it will also run your drill battery down faster.) In each case, take it slow and bear down just enough to feel the drill biting. With a spade bit, the centre point cuts a hole first and if you go too quickly it will melt the acrylic and clog. If it seems like it's not going in, take the drill out and flick the hardened plastic off the cutting surface of the centre point. You will likely need a screwdriver or something hard to do this.

When you break through the first acrylic layer you will know about it because of the feel, but you may find that the drill doesn't want to bite into the lower sheet. Don't be tempted to force it – instead, take the drill out and check the bit. What usually happens is that your bit will have cut a thin 'washer' of acrylic which is now spinning under the drill and preventing it from progressing. With a brad point bit this will usually come out stuck to the centre point and you'll have to prise it off with a screwdriver. With a spade bit, the washer may remain in the hole and you'll have to flip it out, again using a screwdriver or some other implement. Once the hole is clear, re-insert the drill and proceed as before.

Again, you will benefit from trying out these holes on scrap acrylic beforehand. You will find that if you drill too fast, especially with a spade bit, the material melts. This may be okay if you don't stop until you get all the way through, but if you stop and try to re-start you will likely find that the drill judders and you get chips flying because the material had re-solidified irregularly. At worst it will crack, but even at best you may be left with a rough hole, or a hole with a raised lip that you will have to fix with a file. This can end up visible on the finished panel, depending on which kind of component goes in the hole you've messed up. Find the right balance of speed and cutting effectiveness and you won't mess up.

The two-hole tap dance

Once you've cut all the medium-sized holes it's time to do the complex ones. For this you should separate the two acrylic sheets, but not before you have marked up the top and bottom acrylics with the sizes of the holes you need to drill. Once you separate the sheets you will also lose the guide graphic. You know where the holes have to go – you've drilled the 1mm pilot holes, remember – but it's easy to mix up the top and bottom sheets or to mix up the holes, so you want to make sure it's clear.

Once you have the sheets separated you can go on to drill the holes. For the top sheet the procedure is as before – for each panel you will have five 10mm holes to drill, and if you are building the GPS you will have one additional 7mm hole. On the back sheets, the GPS has one 13mm hole and both panels have five 22mm holes. In each case you have a small pilot hole to start you off so there is no problem in locating the drill.

The 22mm holes are more difficult to drill. You will be using a spade bit for these and due to the larger size the resistance to the drill is a lot more than for the smaller holes. All the same cautions apply but you need to take it even slower and be very attentive to the possibility of melting. It is wise to stop from time to time and allow the bit to cool down. In addition, the centre spike will cut a larger hole before the outer spurs make contact with the acrylic and you need to be cautious not to bear down too heavily to avoid cracking. You will very likely get melting on this initial phase of the cut when the main part of the drill begins to make contact make sure you pull it out and clear the centre spike if necessary.

And that should be it! Assuming all has gone well, you can now dust off the two acrylic sheets and when you screw them back together you will have a platform that's ready for mounting the components. It would be wise at this point to test-fit each component in case you have any imperfections that need attention.

Quick-start acrylic panels

There is no denying that cutting and drilling the acrylic sheets is the most difficult part of creating your own panels. It also requires painstaking attention to detail if the results are to bear close scrutiny. If you want to build one of the panels here but you are uncertain about making the acrylics, or if you want to ensure professional quality from the outset, you have the option of buying a quick-start kit from Almost Aviation. The basic quick-start kit is simply a pair of acrylic sheets, either for the GPS or the autopilot. These are professionally laser-cut for a near-perfect finish.

You can find out more about the quick-start kits at www.almostaviation.com.

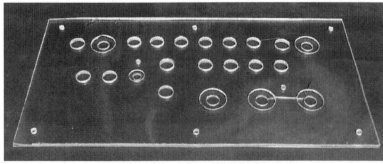

Hand-cut acrylics (GPS shown)

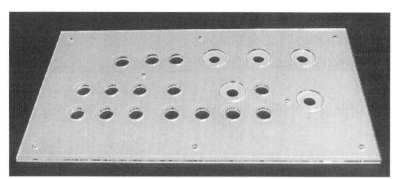

Laser-cut acrylics (autopilot shown)

Hand-cut GPS panel

Laser-cut GPS panel

Printing and mounting the graphics

You have a number of options for creating the graphics, the main decision being whether you choose to print on paper or clear acetate sheets. I will assume you are going to use paper as I have achieved excellent results this way. You can print your graphics on a desktop inkjet or laser printer but with a cheap laser you may find that printing large areas of solid black is problematic. You will also need to decide at this stage whether you are going to want a backlit panel. A single sheet of regular 80gsm printer paper will suffice if you aren't bothered about backlighting, but this is unlikely to be sufficient to prevent bleed-through even in solid black areas for a backlit panel.

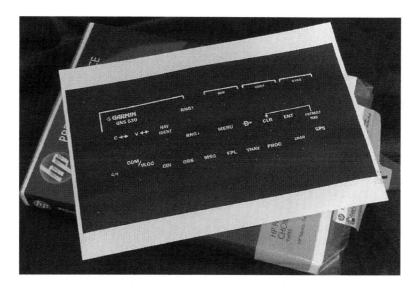

I have chosen to use HP 'Premium Choice' paper, which is bright white 100gsm paper. Again, a single sheet is marginal when building for backlit so I use two sheets with the graphics printed and lined up carefully before mounting. This gives adequate density for backlighting while still allowing good transmission through the white (unprinted) areas. The most important thing when using two sheets is to keep them in perfect registration until they are fixed in position by the mounting screws, otherwise the text and graphics will not be crisp when backlit. It is also crucial to keep the graphics aligned squarely with the edges of the panel, particularly if your graphics include vertical and/or horizontal lines as it will be obvious if they are even slightly skewed. Finally, it is important to trim the edges of the paper accurately to ensure a professional-looking panel. Each of these mounting tasks is addressed below.

Appendix A shows in detail how to create the graphic but from here on I will assume you have managed to print two copies of the final graphic on A4 paper, with slightly extended margins that you will trim to the exact size you need. If you use an inkjet printer to print large areas of colour (or black) you will usually discover that the paper isn't flat but has developed gentle undulations from the wetness of the ink. If you leave it like this the ripples may be visible, although subtly, in the final assembled panel. You can flatten the paper out by pressing it between the pages of a heavy book for a day or two or by ironing it carefully on the back. If you are going to iron it you may want to experiment with a smaller printout first as there is potential for catastrophe. Printing extra copies of a solid black panel will eat up your ink cartridge pretty fast!

The next step is to fix the two sheets together in as near-perfect alignment as is practical. When you sandwich the paper between your two acrylics you will have plenty of overlap all round (the panels are 28cm x 15cm, while an A4 sheet is 29.7cm x 21cm), so the plan is initially to staple them together at the margins. DON'T assume that the image will be positioned exactly the same on each sheet because the printer's paper feed mechanism may well introduce positioning errors. The best way to align the sheets is to stack them together and hold them up to the light, adjusting the alignment by sliding the sheets with a thumb and forefinger until you get the crispest image possible.

Once you have a good alignment, carefully staple the sheets together on the long edges, taking care not to move them while you do so. Once you have the papers stapled together, hold them up to the light again to check the alignment. If it's gone wrong, separate them and do it again until you get it right. You should have plenty of room to re-staple securely as many times as you need. You can also staple at the short ends for extra security. Assuming you have printed the graphic area with over-sized margins, as long as you stay out of the printed area with the staples you won't get in the way of the panel assembly.

To complete the assembly you now need to complete the following steps: sandwich the paper between the acrylic sheets, align it carefully so it is square with the panel edges and all the panel holes are centred over the correct spots (you should have printed cross-hairs for each hole), secure the panels together with the two screws, cut the holes for all the components and trim the edges of the paper to the correct size. The following steps show you a particular logical order in which to do all these things, but you could choose to figure out your own steps instead.

The crucial first step is to lay the topmost acrylic sheet on top of the printed graphic and line it up to get the best registration. At this stage you will need to remove the protective film from one or both sides of you acrylic sheet (some brands have clear film on one side, some have opaque on both sides), so from now on make sure you treat this acrylic carefully because you can mark it. If you have created and printed the graphics perfectly then all you holes should line up with the cross-hairs. Pay special attention to how well your graphics are aligned with the edges of the panel, ensuring that horizontal and vertical lines are parallel with the edges even if this means your holes drift a little away from the centres. A slight discrepancy in the centring of a caption will barely be noticeable, whereas a long printed line that is not parallel to the edge will really stand out. When you have the acrylic and the graphic lined up, fix them with a piece of tape at each edge (use a low-tack tape – this is only temporary).

Now lay this taped pair on top of the second (rearmost) acrylic sheet to complete the sandwich. You won't be able to line them up perfectly as the paper is overhanging, but get them as close as you can. Now carefully make two holes in the paper by poking something sharp through the two fixing holes and enlarging them to the full size of the hole. Fix the sandwich together with two 4mm machine screws and nuts. You can now remove the tape, taking care not to damage the paper.

Although the papers are stapled together you will need to remove the staples when trimming the paper to the size of the panel. This is best done by dismantling the sandwich so you will now introduce an alternative way of maintaining the registration of the two papers. Using a pin, carefully poke a hole through the centre of the top-left and bottom-right mounting holes (the mounting holes are the six 4mm holes at the outside edge of the panel). Make sure you don't enlarge these holes; you want to make sure that re-inserting a pin through the hole will restore the precise registration if need be. You can make holes through all six mounting holes if you want to be extra careful.

The next thing to do is to mark the edges of the paper for cutting, which you should do by running a fine pencil along the paper, using the edge of the acrylic as a ruler. Do this for all four sides, on the front or rear sheet – it will be easier to see on the rear, but arguably the cut will be more accurate if you mark the front. Now dismantle the panel by removing the two screws. Over the next few steps you need to make sure you keep the inside surfaces of your sandwich as free from dust and debris as possible. A good first step is to vacuum (carefully!) the surface of the paper while the two sheets are still stapled together, and also the underside of the acrylic sheet.

For the next step you will need a sharp craft knife and a straight edge. You need to cut precisely and cleanly along the four lines you just marked in pencil, making sure to cut through both sheets of paper. A cut like this is always slightly imprecise, so you should favour cutting very slightly inside the lines so there will be no paper protruding from the sandwich. This step can make or break your panel – use a new blade in your knife if you can, use a metal ruler if you have one and try to make each cut in a single motion. Again, try a few cuts on scrap printouts before attempting the real deal or you may end up needing to start again.

This is the point at which you risk losing registration between your two sheets of paper as you have now cut the staples off! It probably won't happen, but beware of the possibility. When you've made the cuts, carefully reassemble the sandwich, again making sure you have no debris or dust between the paper and the front acrylic. The introduction of dust or debris is perhaps the most annoying part of this whole process and you will need to pay careful attention to this right up to the final assembly. When you come to mounting the assembled (and possibly wired-up) panel it is tempting to drill the six mounting holes using the panel itself as a guide. I strongly recommend NOT doing this, as you can very easily force sawdust in between the panels in the vicinity of the mounting holes and it will look bad. Before you tighten up the two fixing screws, just check the papers have maintained their registration and if not use pins through the pin-holes to restore it.

The final task is to punch out the holes for mounting the components. Again, there are a few ways you could do this, most easily by just cutting two slits in a cross shape through each hole with a sharp knife. I recommend you don't do it this way because you will end up with flaps of paper and these can be problematic. These flaps will make the holes smaller and can make the components a tight fit, but they will also get caught up in the threads when you screw the nuts on to tighten up the components. For the rear-mounted components (rotary encoders), unless you are careful you may also get these paper flaps poking out of the front of the panel, which looks bad.

The method I suggest is to use a pin or a needle and to go around the periphery of each hole poking holes through the paper as close together as you can. This creates a perforated strip which will allow you to punch out a disc of paper leaving minimal debris attached. I suggest you avoid blowing away debris at this stage or you risk introducing dust between the paper and the upper acrylic sheet as described above! Once you have all your holes punched, it's time to install the components.

Wiring up the panel

Wiring up the components is straightforward. All components connect directly to one input each on the controller board (see below for more discussion of the rotary controls). The controller I have used is a Leo Bodnar BBI-32 'Button Box Interface', which has 32 separate inputs, each of which is connected one button or switch. The BBI-32 comes in two variants, one with push-fit connectors and one which requires the connections to be soldered. The push-fit connectors are spring-loaded and very secure; connection is simply a matter of pressing a little tag with a screwdriver or paperclip and inserting the wire. This is the board I would recommend, although if you are on a strict budget the solder version is significantly cheaper.

You could choose instead to use the Leo Bodnar BU0836 board, which also comes in several variants. The main difference is that this has analog inputs as well as the button inputs. (It is also bigger and has different-sized mounting holes.) If you are in the United States and prefer to 'order in', you might choose to use a different controller board, such as the Desktop Aviator 2095A "Sweet 16" or the 2090 Super

Rotary Encoder boards. These are based on the same BU0836 encoder chip as the Leo Bodnar boards. However, please make sure you read the notes on component substitutions in the Appendices, as departing from the specifics of my design may also require you to depart from my instructions and do some more figuring out by yourself.

The components for either of the two boards I have designed are a mixture of simple push-to-make buttons and rotary encoders. The encoders are more complex devices but there is no need to understand their internal workings because they are managed more or less transparently by the controller board. For wiring purposes and, later, for programming purposes, we can treat each rotary encoder as if it were two separate switches, one that 'clicks' when we turn the control to the right (clockwise) and the other that clicks when we turn it to the left (anti-clockwise). These particular components also have a third switch that is activated when we press the knob down. The only constraint is that we must connect each left/right pair (i.e. one for each rotary control) to adjacent inputs on the Bodnar Board (e.g. B1/B2, B3/B4, B31/B32). We also need to tell the controller to expect rotary controls on these inputs, which we do by running the BBI-32 setup program and clicking a few menu options. (This is described in more detail later.)

All the components (rotaries included) are effectively simple push-to-make switches, which means that the switch is normally open and it closes when you activate the component. For push buttons, this means that while you hold the button down its two terminals are connected together. To put it another way, if you wire it into a circuit, pushing the button completes the circuit. If you connect a multi-meter with a continuity tester across the terminals, for example, it will beep when you push the switch. For the rotary controls, you can think of it as each time you turn the knob you get a momentary connection. (If you try this with a multi-meter you will find it isn't that simple, but let's just pretend it is!)

The inputs on the BBI-32 are pairs of connectors and you will notice that one input of each pair is labelled GND. Taking button 1 as an example, you connect one wire from your switch to B1 and the other to GND. Although in principle you could connect two wires from each switch directly to the controller board in this way, it isn't necessary because all the GND connections are wired together – in other words, if you are connected to one GND you are connected to all of them. The implication for us is that we can connect one side of all our switches together behind the panel and then take just one ground wire and connect it to any GND connector on the controller. Then we take independent signal wires from the other terminal of each switch and plug these into the B1, B2, ..., B32 inputs.

Although it is quite possible you could do all of this and make it work without any soldering, I would not recommend this. To get reliable and robust connections for so many switches you really ought to solder the wires. The soldering is not difficult, with the possible exception of the (optional) dual concentric encoder switches, as these are small and the tags are quite delicate and close together. The dual concentric rotaries do come with little circuit boards that make them more robust and easier to connect up, but I have found that soldering the components onto these boards reliably is even trickier than just soldering onto the tags. Don't forget that dual concentric rotaries are not featured in my board designs so you don't need to use them.

Before you begin connecting your wires, please review the following notes on the electrical connections for each component. This will tell you which terminal to connect the ground wire to and which to connect the signal wire to. You will find a complete component list in the appendix, including links to the full specifications.

Square push-buttons

These are as simple as it gets – they have two terminals that are unconnected when the switch is open and which are connected when you press it. You can connect the ground wire to either terminal, it makes no difference.

Round push-buttons

The red buttons are the same as the square buttons – they have two terminals and you can connect the ground to either one.

The black buttons are slightly different – although they look the same these are actually two switches in one, which we can call A and B. This means it has two signal terminals and a common ground. When the switch is up (i.e. you are not pressing it), switch A is open and switch B is closed (connected to the ground terminal). When you press the button, switch A closes and switch B opens. This is called a 'changeover' switch, for obvious reasons, and it is only used here because at the time of designing these panels the equivalent simple switch was not available.

To use this is as a simple switch you need to identify the two terminals that are connected together when you press the switch. You can do this with a multi-meter or other simple continuity tester. (A small battery, a couple of bits of wire and your tongue will make an effective continuity tester!) When you identify the spare terminal you can cut it off or bend it out of the way to avoid confusion. Then it's just the same as the other push-buttons, connect the ground wire to either terminal.

Latching push-button

The GPS panel has a latching push-button for the NAV Ident button. You connect this up just like the other pushbuttons. The only difference is that it latches closed until you press it again.

Rotary controllers

These have five tags, arranged in one group of three and one group of two. This isn't as complicated as it looks – it's just two separate components, one with two tags and one with three. The pair of tags is for connecting the centre-push switch. It works exactly like the push-buttons described above so you can connect the ground wire to either terminal. The group of three tags is arranged with the two signal tags at the outside; the centre tag is a common ground. This means you must connect the ground wire to the centre tag.

Because we are using a common ground for all our components, you will end up with two of the rotary control's tags connected together. This is correct – don't forget, these are actually separate components in a single package.

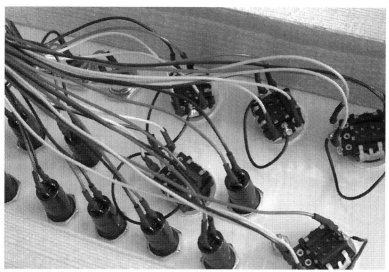
Colour-coded wires will help at the controller end

If you choose to use the optional dual concentric encoders, the principles are just the same but there are a total of five separate switches instead of three. I will not cover the wiring of that component here but you can figure it our with reference to the detailed diagram available on the Leo Bodnar web site.

When connecting the central push-switches for the rotary encoders, you have a choice to make about the wiring. I have designed these boards so that you can wire up the push-switches independently and you will have just enough inputs on the BBI-32 controller board (32) to connect all the components. However, if you stick strictly to my design all the central push-switches will be used for the same function, which is as a SHIFT key to make the rotary knob do two different things according to whether you are pushing it in or not. (See below for a possible exception to this.) And because there is never a situation when you will be holding down more than one rotary knob at the same time, you can (and probably should) choose to wire all the centre push-switches to the same input. This will save you four inputs on each board, which you can then use to connect additional switches or buttons mounted elsewhere.

I would recommend leaving the centre-push of one specific rotary control independent of the others. This is the one intended for adjusting the seat position. Because there will be a mixture of users who have TrackIR, EZCA, both or neither, there are different constraints on how to make the seat adjustment work. Although I have provides SHIFT-aware functions in the library, it makes sense to leave the centre-push available for mapping to a discrete function such as pausing the TrackIR if required. There is a further discussion of this in the section on programming the panels.

Connecting the wires

You will need a supply of suitable wire to makes your connections. If you are using the push-fit Bodnar board you need to choose a wire that is thin enough for the connectors. I used 7/0.2mm wire (seven strands, each strand has a 0.2mm^2 cross-section), which is sold by Maplin by the metre or in 100m spools. A 30W soldering iron with a fine tip will be adequate for connecting the components up. You will find many soldering tutorials on YouTube but honestly you need not bother, soldering to switch tags requires very little finesse.

There are two ways to connect the common ground to all your switches. If you have a source of non-insulated single-core wire (or if you strip some multi-core wire and twist it together) you could run a single wire around (or through the holes in) each terminal and then solder them all up afterwards. Otherwise you will need to connect individual jumper wires between adjacent components until you have all the grounds connected together in a daisy chain. Once you have soldered these you should test for connectivity between the first and last component.

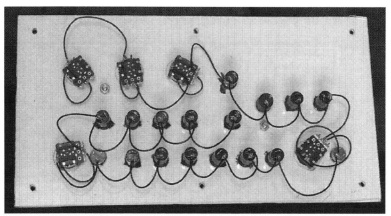

Daisy-chained ground wires can give tidier wiring

There is a third variation of wiring up the common ground. Instead of daisy-chaining the ground connections together, you connect a full-length wire to the ground terminal of each switch. You can then solder them all together at a common point somewhere behind the panel and run your single ground wire to the controller from there. (You could also use a screw-terminal block to avoid soldering.) Or if the controller is mounted close to the panel, you could simply connect all the ground wires independently. The great advantage of this is that you will be able to dismantle the panel later and replace the graphic insert; at worst you will need to de-solder (or cut) at a single point. This is important if you want to be able to change the captions or the panel graphics.

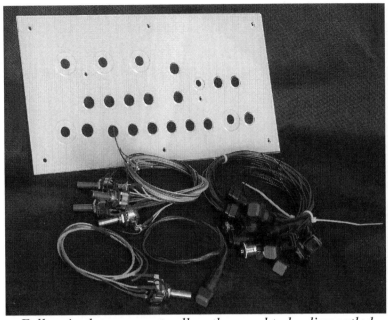

Fully-wired components allow the panel to be dismantled

The push-buttons have holes in their tags so the jumper wires can be secured to the tags for easy soldering once all the wires are in place. I would not recommend soldering these as you go, at least while wiring up the common ground, because you need to connect two wires to each tag to complete the daisy chain and once you solder a tag you've lost the hole! For soldering to the tags on the rotary controllers, I found it best to create a loop at the end of my jumper wire by twisting it around a stretched-out paperclip. This will drop snugly over the pointed bit of the tag if you untwist it slightly and then it will stay in place while you solder it. I do not recommend trying to bend the tags over as you will risk breaking them off.

Mounting the controller board

Before wiring up the signal wires you have some choices to make, notably where you are going to mount the BBI-32 controller board. The board is the size of a credit card, although if you have the one with push-fit connectors it's a lot thicker. It has four holes at the corners which can be used to mount on nylon hex standoff pillars with standard 3mm screws. These bits can all be sourced from Maplin or elsewhere, but they really aren't necessary. There's nothing vulnerable on the back of the board so you can just choose to mount it flush with any suitable (non-conductive) surface and secure it with cable ties (you will need skinny ones). Depending on how you have decided to mount your panel, this might be inside a box or attached to the inside of the panel frame, or somewhere else.

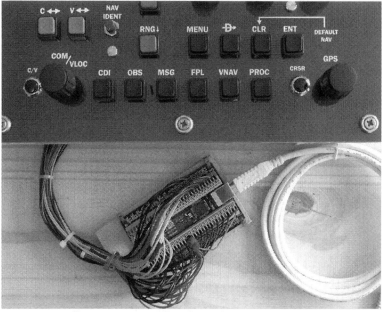

Free-floating controller board (mounted on MDF)

You could choose to mount the controller board in its own box, assuming you can find something about the right size, and have it connected to the panel only by the bundle of wires. Obviously if you do it this way you need to make sure the wires are secured suitably at each end so there is no mechanical load on either the soldered joints at your switches or the Bodnar board connector. In each case, a few cable ties are usually all that's required to secure bundles of wires to something solid. Don't forget that wherever you mount the board you will need a clear path to attach a USB cable to it.

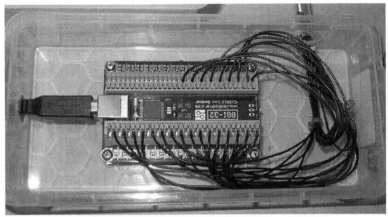

Board mounted on stand-offs in an enclosure

If you are really ambitious, and especially if you plan to build more and bigger panels, you might choose to mount your controller boards in a single cabinet, remotely from the panels. For larger projects such as this you should really consider making your panels detachable and use umbilical cables to connect them to the controller cabinet. Once you have connected the wires up to the controller – and especially after you have done your programming – you do not want to be removing thirty-odd wires if you want to take a board out and tinker with it, particularly as you will have to re-connect all the wires to the same inputs when you re-attach it.

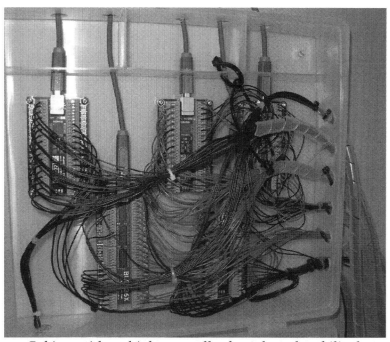

Cabinet with multiple controller boards and umbilicals

There are as many solutions to this kind of problem as there are types of connector. For my Twin Otter cockpit I used 25-way D-type connectors, which are traditionally used for RS-232 cables. These have pins which are big enough to solder onto fairly easily. You will need two of these to ensure enough connectors for each of the panels described here, and this means you will need two pairs of male and female connectors and four covers to make a complete umbilical, assuming it's hard-wired at the controller end. (There is little need to make a completely detachable cable unless you are a real purist, or perhaps are going to be moving your controller cabinet around a lot.) Making detachable panels requires a lot of extra soldering, but it is definitely worth the effort if you are building an extensive panel.

25-way D-Sub connector for umbilical

Whichever solution you choose for mounting the controller board will determine how long your signal wires need to be. Once you have established that, you can solder them onto the free terminals of the switches and bundle them up into a neat cable with a bunch of cable ties or something similar. (Don't forget to connect the signal wires from each of the five rotary encoders together, unless you have chosen to wire them independently. You can do this by wiring a 'daisy-chain' between them like you did for the ground connections and then taking one signal wire out in your exit bundle.) You will need to solder one wire onto the ground daisy-chain and it makes sense to use a different coloured wire for this so it is easily identifiable when you come to connect the wires to the controller.

You also need to make sure that the pairs of left/right wires from the rotary controls are identifiable as pairs, since as described earlier you will need to plug these into adjacent inputs on the controller. I used short lengths of heat-shrink tubing near the controller end, but you can use cable ties or even sticky tape (not recommended unless you like things sticky). Other than that, there is no need to identify the individual signals as it is immaterial which inputs they are connected to. Then it's just a matter of stripping the ends of the wires and connecting them up to the BBI-32!

Setting up the BBI-32 board

When you buy the BBI-32 board it doesn't come with any software or instructions so it isn't immediately obvious that you need to do anything beyond plugging the wires in. (Although to be fair, if you read the product page carefully it tells you all you need to know.) Indeed, if all you plug in are simple switches and buttons there is nothing else to do. Windows will detect the board as a game controller as soon as you plug it into a USB port and you will be able to experiment with it using the game controller settings dialogs in Windows Control Panel.

If you are plugging rotary encoders into you BBI-32 (you are) then you need to download and run the configuration program and tell it which pairs of inputs you have connected rotary encoders to. For each pair of inputs there is a drop-down list, which initially has OFF selected. Assuming you are using the encoders I have specified, you should choose 1:1 from the list, which means you will get one pulse (momentary button press) for each détente. (You can experiment with the other settings and the Control Panel game controller dialog to see what they do.) By the way, you will notice that the BBI-32 configuration program displays the serial number of the BBI-32 board and it's a good idea to write this down somewhere. If you plug in another BBI-32 board this is the only way to distinguish them and if you are building a complex cockpit it gets confusing very fast (trust me, I have six controllers). For any pairs of inputs that don't have rotary encoders connected, just leave them set to OFF. You shouldn't need to change any of the other parameters on the setup program.

Software matters

Checking out the panel

Sooner or later you will end up with a finished panel with all
the components wired up and connected to the controller
board. Depending on how ambitious your design is, this may
include extra solder connections and an umbilical cable, which
you all need to be checked out end to end to ensure your
connections are good. Once you have plugged the controller
into a USB port on your PC you can check these out
systematically using the game controller settings dialogs in
Windows Control Panel.

The simplest way is to just go across the board and push each
switch in turn, checking that it appears in the dialog as a
unique button event. This includes the rotary encoders which,
assuming you have correctly set up the controller board as
described earlier, behave just like momentary button clicks.
There is no need to note which switch on the panel
corresponds to which number in the settings dialog, other than
to ensure that each activates a different number! (But
remember that if you use the common wiring for the rotary
knob SHIFT function, the centre push-switch of each rotary
knob will activate the same button click.)

Quick start

To make these panels work as I have designed them you will
need to install a registered copy of FSUIPC and the freeware
program LINDA, which makes FSUIPC much easier to use.
FSUIPC is available from
http://www.schiratti.com/dowson.html, and LINDA from
www.fs-linda.com. FSUIPC can be installed as freeware, but

45

its functionality will remain limited until you purchase a licence for it. You will not be able to program buttons and switches with the unregistered version of FSUIPC, nor will you be able to use LINDA.

Assuming you have these programs installed, all you need to do is to copy the Almost Aviation LINDA library file to the appropriate folder (\Microsoft Flight Simulator X\modules\linda\libs) and all the functions you need will appear in the LINDA menus. You can then map library functions to the button and switches. Although LINDA is fairly intuitive up to a point, it's perhaps fair to recognise that your intuition is not my intuition and so I have provided a complete walk-through of the steps needed to program the GPS panel in the appendices.

If you are going to change the functions that you attach to the buttons and switches on the panels you may need to look a little deeper into the internals of the LINDA files. This is particularly true of the Autopilot panel, as this has extra buttons on it that you may wish to use for different purposes to the ones I have chosen. By default I have reserved these for the TrackIR and seat position, which you may not want (or may not be able) to use. The information in the next section will be helpful in understanding a bit more about how to do this.

Advanced information for experimenters

I'm going to use the F-word

You will already know that a registered copy of FSUIPC is a requirement to get the full functionality of these panels. I won't go into FSUIPC in great detail because it does a lot of useful things and the scope is huge, but for our purposes it is an FSX add-on that provides ways of hooking up hardware buttons and switches to FSX functions. You may wonder why we need that because at first glance it duplicates something we can already do in the Options/Settings/Controls dialog within FSX. But when you look more closely you discover that this is only partially true and the closer you look, the clearer it becomes that FSX can't do all we need it to.

To take an example, many of the functions in FSX are manipulated by invoking functions called 'selection increase' and 'selection decrease', which are mapped to the '=' and '-' keys by default. These do different things according to where FSX has its focus directed and they are used to make many complex adjustments in FSX – setting the radio frequencies, selecting the OBS on the VOR and so on – in combination with functions that move the focus onto the control to be adjusted. To set the OBS (omni-bearing selector) for VOR1, for example, you first need to invoke the 'select OBS' function and then repeatedly invoke 'selection increase' and/or 'selection decrease' to move the OBS. If you call up the controls dialog within FSX you'll find a long list of functions that you can hook up to buttons or keys, but you will quickly discover that you can't do something like manipulate the OBS with just two buttons (or a rotary encoder) for increase/decrease because in each case you need to make sure the OBS is selected first and there is no way to invoke two functions from one button.

It's actually a lot worse than that, but it will suffice to say that to get full access to all of FSX's internal functions – and without the limitations of FSX's button-mapping and key-mapping dialog – you need FSUIPC. Inside FSUIPC you will find a similar dialog and a familiar list of FSX functions that can be hooked up to buttons and keys directly, without the need to move the focus between controls first. You will also discover that it is a bigger list of functions than appears in the FSX Options/Settings/Controls dialog. There are a number of reasons for this which need not concern us here. It is enough to say that all the functions you will ever need to directly invoke standard FSX 'Event Ids' (as they are called in the FSX SDK documentation) are listed here, and a few more besides. You can read all about this in great detail in the FSUIPC documentation, which is available for free from the FSUIPC support forums at simFlight.

As you will see in the next section I will be using another tool to drive FSUIPC and so I won't be saying too much more about the details of programming buttons and switches in directly FSUIPC. However, you could choose to do all of your programming in FSUIPC and you will still be able to fully implement the panels as I designed them. The main thing you will need to figure out is how to do compound button controls, which means making the action of a button conditional in the setting of another button. This is explained in the guide 'FSUIPC for Advanced Users', which comes with the product (or can be downloaded for free) and it is one way to implement the SHIFT function for the rotary controls. The reason(s) we need a SHIFT function may not yet be obvious, but that will become clear when we look at the individual functions.

And now, the L-words

The next thing you'll need is LINDA, a program designed to hide the arcane workings of FSUIPC with something simpler. LINDA is a free download from www.fs-linda.com and you can read more about at in the support forums at Avsim. LINDA builds on a particular subset of FSUIPC's capabilities to give you a friendly and intuitive way to make FSX do what you want when you flip buttons and switches. Here's an example. Let's say you want to program a toggle switch to control your landing gear. Assuming you have FSUIPC installed and LINDA is running, all you do is flip the switch you want to control the landing gear, choose the 'drop landing gear' function from a menu and you're done. I've left out a few steps, but that's basically it. With LINDA installed, it runs automatically with FSX and at its simplest, it allows you to program your panel simply by flipping the switches and choosing functions from menus. Once you have your buttons and switches programmed LINDA remembers your settings independently for each aircraft you fly.

You may have noticed the phrase 'at its simplest' in the description above and that's because LINDA can do a lot of other things too. One of the FSUIPC features it builds on is its scripting engine, which allows you to create more complex actions and attach them to your buttons and switches. You don't have to get into this but because LINDA uses it behind the scenes to do all of its button mapping, other people can share their work in libraries that you can simply plug in to LINDA and use. For example, if you visit the LINDA download forum you will find many freely-available libraries that allow you to map functions in such diverse FSX aircraft as the Aerosoft Twin Otter Extended, A2A Cessna Skylane and several of the PMDG airliners to your panels. One thing all of those aircraft have in common is that they rely heavily on custom-built functions that cannot be invoked directly from FSX.

Scripts in FSUIPC (and therefore in LINDA) are written in a programming language called Lua. If you use Windows Explorer to poke around in the FSX\Modules folder (which is where FSUIPC and LINDA install themselves) you will likely see a number of files with the extension '.lua', and these are Lua source files. They are simple text files that you can open with programs such as Notepad to have a look at. I am making certain assumptions here about how technically-minded you are, including how well-versed you may be in Windows arcana. My rationale is that since you are reading this, you are at least considering embarking on a fairly technical project!

However, knowledge of Windows and experience of technical matters are not essential for you to succeed with a project such as this, but it's fair to say that non-technical readers will find the learning curve a bit steeper.

With that in mind, if you are finding it difficult to track these '.lua' files down (or don't know what I mean by a file extension), now would be a good time to make sure you have the 'Hide extensions for known file types' option in Windows Explorer's 'Folder options...' dialog. This is one of the more regrettable defaults in recent versions of Windows that tries to shield users from technical matters. I will not explain in detail how to change this, but for Windows 7 you will find it in Control Panel under 'Folder Options'. It is likely that even now some of you are trying to find this option in Internet Explorer instead of Windows Explorer, which will do you no good at all. You are looking for files on your computer, not web pages, so the tool of choice is Windows Explorer. You can find it on the Start menu under All programs/Accessories (or you can run it by double-clicking the My Computer icon if you have one on your desktop).

If you found any of that stuff about Windows files difficult, it is likely that you are not a programmer and so you will probably find Lua a bit scary. For most purposes you will not need to know about what is inside a Lua file, you will only need to know how to copy files around and where to put a 'something.lua' file you get from elsewhere. However, for more advanced tweaking of your panels you will occasionally need to open up a Lua file and poke around in it. Mostly you can do this by looking at what other people have done and making simple changes or additions of your own, but if you know (or can figure out) what you are doing you will be able to do lots more. There are two places to look for information you need to make full use of Lua. These are the FSUIPC documentation, and the Lua language reference materials.

Advanced users may also want to look at the FSUIPC SDK, available from www.schiratti.com/dowson.html. (This is not the same thing as the FSX SDK.)

An aside – Lua scripts, FSUIPC and LINDA

If you remember back to the earlier discussion of how to link buttons and switches to FSX internal functions (which the FSX SDK calls 'Event IDs') you will recall that there is a list of these inside the FSUIPC dialog, which you can find when you open up FSUIPC from the Addons menu in FSX. This list has more things on it than the functions listed in FSX's own 'Options/Setting/Controls' screen, but the really interesting thing is that you can add more things to it by writing Lua scripts. Essentially, if you put a file called 'myprogram.lua' in the right place, you will see a new entry 'myprogram' (actually it will say 'Lua:myprogram') in FSUIPC's function list and you can link this to a button press just like a regular FSX function.

One of the most common reasons for writing Lua programs like this is to poke around inside of custom aircraft models to discover publicly-accessible Gauge Local Variables (also known as Lvars). This is the magic that allows us to interface our controls to models like the A2A Skylane or Aerosoft Twin Otter Extended, which don't rely on standard FSX functionality. You won't need Lvars to make the GPS and Autopilot panels work as designed but it's helpful to know they exist because if you open up any of the Lua files that come with LINDA you're going to see many references to Lvars. You may, of course, choose to program your GPS and Autopilot panels differently to how I have designed them, in which case you may or may not need to get involved with Lvars.

LINDA uses Lua in a slightly different way but it's similar in general concept. I will describe the LINDA folder structure in detail later, but for now it's enough to know that LINDA can associate a single Lua file with any given aircraft. That file generally contains the definitions of public functions that will appear in the LINDA menus (e.g. 'A2A Spitfire/Electrics/SPIT APU On') and that can, therefore, be bound to buttons and switches. The LINDA menus also allow you to access all the built-in FSX functions too, so in fact you can program all the default aircraft (and likely some simpler payware ones too) without recourse to Lua functions at all. Well, almost.

Why almost? Well, one reason to use Lua would be to implement compound button controls, which you may remember were mentioned earlier in the discussion of FSUIPC. To take an example, to make the rotary encoders work with the GPS we need to be able to do different things with the inputs depending on whether the central push-switch is held down or not. This means we can distinguish between group switching (push-and-turn) and page switching (turn). Essentially this uses the push-switch as a SHIFT key, which lets us call two different functions depending on whether the SHIFT key is pressed or not.

You will find that LINDA has a method for implementing SHIFT functions already, but reports from users suggest that this is not problem-free and so we're not going to use it. It is in any case straightforward to implement a SHIFT key independently using Lua, which is what I have done. From the user's point of view this is simpler to use – you will find a pair of functions (left/right) for each rotary control and an additional pair of functions (Rotary Shift ON, Rotary Shift OFF) to map to the centre-push button's Down and Up events. The logic that makes sense of these conditions is hidden inside the Lua functions and you don't need to know about it – all you do is map the left/right/push actions to the functions provided in the Almost Aviation LINDA library. (Don't worry if this description is a bit vague, you will see exactly what to do in the programming walk-through for the GPS panel.)

There are other things we can do with Lua that aren't otherwise possible. Consider as an example the Garmin GNS530, as implemented in the Aerosoft Twin Otter Extended. The Twin Otter simulates the real GNS530 using the default GPS500 in combination with the COM1 and NAV1 radios. One consequence of this is that the COM/VLOC toggle isn't implemented directly and so in order to know whether the left-hand rotary control is changing the COM frequency or the NAV frequency we need to keep track of this ourselves. Again, this is easy to do with a simple Lua program that uses a variable to keep track of the mode (COM or VLOC).

If you want to study the details of how the SHIFT or COM/VLOC toggle are implemented you can look at the Almost Aviation library file, which is well-commented. You should read both the LINDA manual and the Advanced (but not very!) Manual, both available at www.fs-linda.com, which explain very clearly how to use LINDA. You may also find it instructive to look through the LINDA libraries supplied and for more advanced ideas, the Lua examples in the FSUIPC documents folder (FSX\modules\FSUIPC Documents).

The LINDA folder structure

Although you may not need to look inside Lua files it is helpful to understand the layout of the LINDA folder tree, which 'grows' downwards from the FSX\modules folder. In fact it's two trees, with the root folders 'linda' and Linda-cfg'. The first is the one we're more interested in, as it contains all the Lua code for actually *doing* stuff. The other tree ('linda-cfg') is where LINDA remembers what joysticks and controllers you have installed and what functions you have linked to which buttons and switches on each one.

Here is a partial structure of the 'linda' folder tree:

```
\fsx\modules\linda
    \aircrafts
        A2A B17
        A2A Cessna C172R
        ...
        (etc.)
    \libs
        lib-AlmostAviation.lua
        ...
        lib-fsx.lua
        lib-realityxp.lua
        ...
        (etc.)
```

There are other sub-folders but you don't need to worry so much about those. The 'aircrafts' folder is where you will find a sub-folder for each aircraft that has a LINDA library installed. You get many of these when you download LINDA but you can add more as they are developed by simply copying them in from the zip files you download from the LINDA Downloads forum. In each aircraft sub-folder you will find three files, but the one you're interested in is 'actions.lua'. This contains the functions that will appear in the LINDA menus and you can browse through it or even add your own functions when you figure out how.

You will find that when LINDA starts it recognises the aircraft you currently have loaded up in FSX and selects the appropriate aircraft-specific library. You can change this manually, but you will find that it is only possible to show the functions from one aircraft-specific library at a time on the LINDA menu. This means that you can't program your switches with a mix and match of functions from, say, the

A2A Spitfire and the Aerosoft Catalina. (Which usually wouldn't make sense anyway.)

The other important sub-folder in the Linda folder is 'libs', which is just a another place the put Lua programs. It makes sense to put a file here if it is useful across more than one aircraft, and you will find things in here for driving the RealityXP GPS and Weather Radar products, various VR Insight panels and for accessing the FSX default functions. This is also where you will put the Almost Aviation library that contains the functions you will need to hook up to the GPS and Autopilot panels. (If you are reading this on the Kindle book you will need to create this file by copying and pasting the text. You will find the text and instructions for doing this in the appendices.)

LINDA – hints for programmers

Although Lua is a simple programming language, it's not *that* simple and it would be unreasonable to imagine I could teach it to you here even if I were proficient in it myself. The basics are easy to pick up if you have any programming experience but I will just note here a few things I have discovered about how LINDA uses Lua that will be helpful to get you started. This section is written for people who are already programmers or at least have some understanding of programming.

If you examine one of the aircraft-specific 'actions.lua' files installed by LINDA you will discover that it is generally just a collection of function definitions, which are chunks of executable Lua code contained between the keywords 'function' and 'end'. The same goes for the library files you will find in \linda\libs, which are named with the format 'lib-something.lua'.

What may not be immediately obvious is that these files can also contain executable Lua code that is not within a function definition. In fact on startup, the 'actions.lua' file for the selected aircraft is loaded and all the statements in it are executed from top to bottom. When a function definition is 'executed' it just defines the function, it doesn't execute the code within it. In other words it stores that chunk of code somewhere and attaches a name to it that can then be used in other Lua code to call that function and run the code inside it. All the library files are loaded and executed at this point too.

Any code that isn't inside a function definition will execute immediately when actions.lua (or, say, the Almost Aviation library file) is loaded. In fact if you examine the library files you will notice that most have a statement of the form '_log("Almost Aviation Library loaded…")' as the last thing in the file. This is a debugging aid that writes to the LINDA Console window so you can see that the libraries have loaded.

One way this is useful is to define and initialise variables that you want to share between functions in the file and you can see an example of this in the flag that tracks whether or not the SHIFT key for the rotary controls is currently held down. In the Almost Aviation library, this variable is defined like this:

```
local RotaryShiftActive = 0
```

This defines the variable and initialises it to 0, which any functions that check this flag will interpret as False (i.e. SHIFT is not active). It is then manipulated by a pair of functions bound to the up and down actions of the push-switches on the rotary encoder knobs. Note the word 'local', which means this variable is not visible outside of this source file. Variables defined without the 'local' keyword are implicitly global, which means they will be visible in all the other library files. This has implications for using a name that is already in use in other Lua code and it can lead to unexpected results. It's also worth pointing out that naming clashes are the same for functions as they are for variables, so it's important to name your functions in a way that's likely to be unique. (This is why all the Almost Aviation library functions are prefixed with 'AAL_'.)

Although the Lua files are executed once on startup, any functions and variables defined in 'actions.lua' or the library files persist for the life of your FSX session. This means, for example, that you can define a global variable and it will continue to exist so that you can use it from your own functions.

The messy world of FSX controller mapping

You can treat this section as background reading (or skip it altogether) unless you are having particular difficulties with your buttons and switches. The information here will serve as a roadmap if you need to get into problem-solving.

You have probably discovered that when you connect a new joystick or game controller to your computer, FSX has a go at mapping some functions to it. This sometimes helps but you will typically end up with unexpected button mappings and perhaps conflicting axes (more than one axis mapped to the same function) too. You are probably also familiar with situations where you makes changes to your button mappings, perhaps to delete such conflicts, and quit FSX only to find the changes have not been saved.

FSX keeps track of the mapping of game controller axes, buttons and switches in file called standard.xml. You will find two copies of this file, one in
\users\yourname\AppData\Roaming\Microsoft\FSX\Controls and one in your main FSX folder. The former is the active one

and you will notice it may be updated when you quite FSX. In fact, if you plug in a new BBI-32 board, start FSX and then quit, you will discover a whole new section named 'Button Box Interface', with some default mappings applied.

If you read about standard.xml you can discover how to edit it manually and/or how to create a default version of your own so your mappings don't get lost. However, given that you are using FSUIPC and LINDA there is a much simpler solution, which is to go into the FSX Options/Settings/Controls screen and de-select the 'enable controllers' check box. This means you will no longer be using FSX to map your controls, so standard.xml is irrelevant.

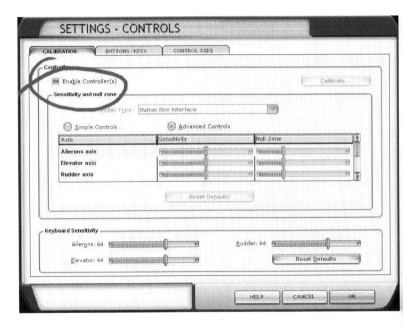

That aside, you may still encounter issues with multiple controllers. To a large degree this depends on what add-ons you use and whether they address your game controllers. On my setup, aside from FSX itself, add-ons that know about game controllers are FSUIPC, LINDA, EZCA, TrackIR and

SPAD. (EZCA is the EzDok Camera Addon and SPAD is the Saitek Advanced Panel Driver.) Unless you approach things methodically this can lead to conflicting mappings of the same buttons, axes and keys in different programs.

You can read about how FSUIPC manages multiple controllers in the FSUIPC User Guide but the basic recommendation is to ensure your fsuipc4.ini file (which you will find in \fsxfolder\modules) has the following entry:

```
[JoyNames]
AutoAssignLetters=Yes
```

In this way FSUIPC avoids tracks each controller uniquely and avoids the migration of programmed buttons from one controller to another when devices are added or removed. However, when you start plugging multiple controllers into LINDA you will potentially have similar difficulties. To minimise problems it is important to names your controllers individually as LINDA by default will only display the 'friendly' device name. (When you have six devices all named 'Button Box Controller', the friendliness wears off pretty quickly!) Check the LINDA manual for details, or just tinker with it in the 'Setup Joysticks' page (it isn't difficult to figure out).

I would advise you to plug all of your controllers in before you program any of them with LINDA. If you are building both the GPS and the Autopilot panel this will be two BBI-32 controllers. If you don't do this, you may find that plugging a new controller in (or unplugging one) makes the programmed buttons disappear. In fact they don't disappear but LINDA gets confused about which controller is which and you will find your actions are now triggered by the buttons connected to a different controller. If this happens to you *can* sort it out but you will need to edit the files under \fsx\modules\linda-cfg\aircrafts\ and essentially switch the joystick identifiers around. I will not go into that here as it is much better to avoid the problem in the first place. In any case you can always just re-program the buttons from scratch if required. It should be a very rare occurrence and will not be too laborious if you only have a couple of panels.

EZCA users

If you use EZCA to manage your views you will discover that it is a prime offender in its inability to manage multiple controllers. This means that you may not be able to map EZCA functions to the buttons you want to use because when you press them EZCA doesn't see the buttons. Fortunately EZCA also lets you map key combinations (e.g. CTRL+X and so on) and you can use FSUIPC (and that means LINDA too) to send keystrokes when a button is pressed.

Although this may sound circuitous it is very reliable in practice. Incidentally, mapping keystrokes to buttons is also the way the Reality XP GPS works and if you want to see how to send keystrokes from Lua code you can open up the RXP library in \fsx\modules\linda\libs\lib-realityxp.lua. If you use EZCA and want to avoid any Lua entanglements you may wish to map your key combinations to buttons using FSUIPC directly rather than with LINDA. (I will say more about this in the section on programming the panels.)

The Almost Aviation library

The Lua source code for the Almost Aviation library is listed in Appendix C. You don't need to look at this if you don't want to but if for any reason you can't download the file you will be able to reconstruct it from the text in Appendix C. You will also find instructions there for doing so.

The Almost Aviation library is a LINDA library file that you need to copy to the folder \fsx\modules\linda\libs, as described earlier. Once you have done this the library is 'installed' and ready to go. When you start LINDA and go to the screen where you map function to buttons you will now discover a new library called 'LIB: Almost Aviation' and under this a collection of functions with names grouped under a number of headings. I will outline these briefly below, but hopefully they will make sense even without any explanation.

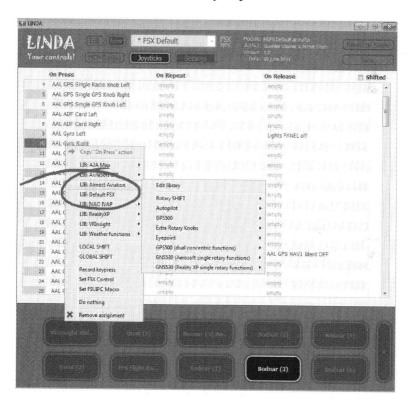

There are three main sub-menus which contain functions for the Autopilot, GPS and extra rotary controls. If you are only building one of the panels not all of these menus will be applicable so you can just ignore the ones that you don't need. You will also see two extra menus called Rotary SHIFT and

61

Eyepoint. The first of these contains the two functions you will need to map to the centre-push switch of most of the rotary controls. Don't forget that you will need to map the ON function to the down action of the switch and the OFF function to the up action. (If you find that SHIFT seems to get stuck on you have likely missed out an OFF action on one of the rotary controls.) The Eyepoint menu provides functions for mapping to the rotary knob I have labelled 'Seat Position' in the sample graphics. (I will say more about these functions later.)

Finally, you will notice three more sub-menus. One of these contains the alternative functions you will need if you choose to build your GPS with dual concentric rotary controls instead of the single ones. The other two contain functions you will need if you have either the Reality XP GNS530 GPS or the Aerosoft Twin Otter Extended, since that aircraft has a simplified version of the GNS530 built in. These functions really belong in the LINDA files for those specific add-ons but I have included them here for convenience (and because I don't own those two files). In fact you will find that these menus only contain the missing functions for using the single rotary controls on my panels, so if you had those products you would map most of the buttons to the functions in the other LINDA libraries (which you would find in, respectively, \fsx\modules\linda\libs\lib-realityxp.lua and \fsx\modules\linda\aicrafts\Aerosoft_DHC6\actions.lua.

Using the Almost Aviation library

You don't actually *need* the library at all. You could choose to program your panel entirely with FSUIPC, in which case you would not need LINDA or the Almost Aviation library. Even using LINDA, you will find that many of the Lua functions simply invoke the default FSX functions directly and there are other ways of doing this with LINDA. For example, you could choose to map almost all of the G500 GPS functions by choosing the functions from LINDA's 'LIB: Default FSX' library or alternatively by using the 'Set FSX Control' menu option. However, you would need to rely on LINDA's SHIFT functions to distinguish between the shifted and un-shifted rotary controls and, as I suggested earlier, this appears to be unreliable in practice (some people have found that the SHIFT function can get stuck on for no good reason).

That said, I have collected the functions together in one place and given them what I hope are friendlier names, or perhaps names that are more clearly connected to the buttons I expect you to link them to on my panels. I have also made a few changes, not least of which is that I have implemented the SHIFT function independently of LINDA. This means you just need to link a left/right pair of functions to each rotary control and then make sure you map the rotary control's push switch to the SHIFT functions as described earlier. The only real differences are that I have changed the behaviour of the default Altitude Hold function to add an ARM function, I have added a function to toggle the autopilot wing-leveler and I have included functions that will allow you to add the COM1/NAV1 radio management to the default GPS, like on the GNS530. (This latter is constrained by there being no visible indication of which radio you are tuning, other than watching which radio changes when you turn the knobs, so I have included an option to show a brief indication in a pop-up window when you press the NAV1/COM1 toggle.)

Of course, as delivered the Almost Aviation library only generates calls to default FSX functions. This means that it may not be sufficient to hook up the autopilot panel to any particular add-on aircraft you may have. This is no different from any other generic controller such as you can buy from Saitek, VR Insight, GoFlight and so on. With complex add-on aircraft you will typically find that some of the functions work but that some are custom-implemented within the model and hence don't respond to the standard FSX commands.

For such add-on aircraft you will need to figure out how to hook into these custom functions – or find out if someone has done it already! This is where LINDA comes into its own as it makes the task simple enough that you will likely find your aircraft has already been supported by someone else. Even if not, LINDA has an excellent 'tracer' tool that helps make the job reasonably easy. You can visit the LINDA support forums to look at which aircraft are supported and for help with implementing functions for your aircraft. You can also discuss the business of building or modifying LINDA functions in the forum at www.almostaviation.com.

Incidentally, the above limitation doesn't apply to the GPS as you can install the G500 GPS 2D panel (or indeed the hand-held GPS295 if you prefer) in any add-on aircraft simply by adding a few lines to that aircraft's panel.cfg file. This means you will always be able to use the default FSX GPS with your Almost Aviation panel. Of course if the aircraft comes with a custom GPS – or you have bought a GPS product such as the GNS430 or GNS530 from Reality XP or Mindstar – you will likely want to put some time into getting that one working with the panel instead.

Programming the panels

Although I have used the word 'programming', hooking up your panels is simply a matter of selecting which functions from the Almost Aviation library you want to attach to each switch. You achieve this by clicking the menus in LINDA and this is sufficiently intuitive that it almost requires no instructions. However, I will comment briefly on the process here. As I have said elsewhere, this will only be the case for aircraft that use the standard FSX GPS and autopilot functions. If you want to use an add-on aircraft that implements (wholly or partially) GPS or autopilot functions internally you will need to figure out how to access those functions, if indeed it is possible to do so. This will be the case for any other hardware panel you can buy. I will not cover such matters here but you will find a wealth of useful information in the LINDA manuals and by browsing or asking in the LINDA support forums.

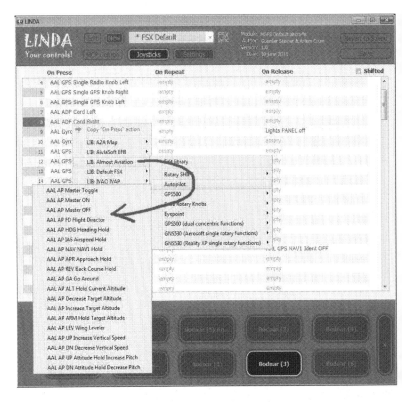

TrackIR and EZCA controls

I have included controls on the autopilot panel for adjusting
the eyepoint and for controlling the TrackIR. If you don't use a
TrackIR you will likely reassign the two TrackIR buttons for
other purposes, but if you do want the TrackIR buttons you
will need to know that the functions I have provided work by
generating keystrokes. These are aimed at the TrackIR driver
and you will be familiar with having to press keys to pause and
re-centre your TrackIR. However, it is very likely that I am not
generating the keystrokes you have set up so you will need to
change something.

You have the option of changing your TrackIR settings to
respond to the keystrokes I generate or of editing the functions

in *lib-Almost Aviation.lua* to generate the specific keystrokes you have set up. (These are defined in the 'hotkeys' section of the TrackIR profile screen, which is under 'Advanced Settings' in the TrackIR user interface.) If you prefer to do the latter you can find a convenient map of how to generate the keystrokes in *lib-realityxp.lua*. I will list a table of all the keystrokes I have hard-coded at the end of this section. The only editing you will need to do to the Lua code is to change the numbers in the *ipc.keypress* calls.

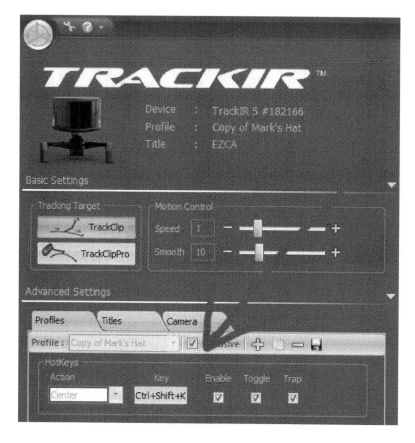

I have found it extremely useful to build a seat adjustment (a.k.a. eyepoint adjustment) control into my panels and I have included a rotary knob for this purpose on the autopilot panel.

It is difficult to cater for everyone here as there will be people out there using different combinations of TrackIR and EZCA, including neither or both. I have supplied separate functions that address the eyepoint adjustment functions of FSX and EZCA and I would also suggest that you leave the centre-push switch of the seat adjustment rotary control independent of the other rotary controls when you wire it up. This will allow more flexibility in the assignment of functions, particularly if you do not have EZCA.

The most satisfactory setup will be one with TrackIR and EZCA. EZCA installs itself to intercept the TrackIR actions, which allows it to insert its own effects. These are chiefly camera movements but it also allows the 'home' eyepoint to be moved independently of TrackIR and the functions for doing so can be bound to buttons or keystrokes. (Again, I have used keystrokes as EZCA evidently cannot handle more than one BBI-32 interface card.) As when switching cameras in EZCA, the movement is rather elegantly damped so that the seat adjustments are smooth and unobtrusive.

EZCA VIEW SYSTEM

	Keyboard	Joystick
Forward	Ctr+Up	
Backward	Ctr+Down	
Left	Ctr+PageUp	
Right	Ctr+PageDown	
Up	Ctr+Right	
Down	Ctr+Left	
Acceleration 1	Ctr+Num 1	
Acceleration 2	Ctr+Num 4	
Global enable		J2 Btn 10
Edit mode	Ctr+Num 2	
Show main form	Sht+ D	

Cycle view

Next camera	Ctr+Sht+Right	
Previous camera	Ctr+Sht+Left	
Next category		
Previous category		

Emulate MM button		

Mode ● T ○ H

DEFAULT VIEW SYSTEM

	Keyboard	Joystick
Next in current category		
Prev. in current category		
Next category		
Prev. category		

Users with EZCA but no TrackIR can use the same functions to the good effect, while those without either EZCA or

69

TrackIR will instead need to use the FSX eyepoint adjustment functions. The Almost Aviation library provides both options and I have also made them SHIFT-aware. You will find that the functions come in pairs – for example, EZCA_Eyepoint_Down_Or_Back() and EZCA_Eyepoint_Up_Or_Forward() – which denote the different actions on shifted and un-shifted operation of the knob. You have the option, therefore, of mapping the centre-push switch to the SHIFT functions as for all the other rotary controls, or to use it for something else – perhaps to reset the eyepoint, for example. In this case the knob always performs the un-shifted action, which will always be the Up/Down one. For the functions Eyepoint_Up() and Eyepoint_Down(), the SHIFT key determines whether the adjustment is coarse or fine.

Unfortunately I have not found a way to move the home eyepoint when TrackIR is used without EZCA. This seriously limits the usefulness of a seat adjustment control and inevitably leads to some compromises. Essentially, any seat (eyepoint) adjustments are now temporary and can only be made when the TrackIR is paused. The most obvious solution is to combine seat adjustments with the pause function and one way is to map the centre-push operation to pause the TrackIR (the function actually toggles the TrackIR on and off).

This gives you a somewhat convenient way to peek over the dash when you need to (on the approach, say) and the eyepoint snaps back when you un-pause the TrackIR. You have a choice of whether the centre-push switch toggles the TrackIR back on when you release the button or whether it leaves it paused until you press it again, making for two quite different operations in practice. Note that you will also lose the option of back/forward or left/right movements if you use the centre-push switch in this way.

These are the keystrokes I have hard-coded for controlling the EZCA and TrackIR functions:

TrackIR Pause:	CTRL + SHIFT + K
TrackIR Centre:	CTRL + SHIFT + Q
EZCA Back:	CTRL + Down Arrow
EZCA Forward:	CTRL + Up Arrow
EZCA Up:	CTRL + Right Arrow
EZCA Down:	CTRL + Left Arrow
EZCA Left:	CTRL + PgUp
EZCA Right:	CTRL + PgDown

Appendix A: Creating the graphics

You can get template files for the graphics from www.almostaviation.com in a number of formats. If for any reason you are unable to get these files or to use them, you can create the graphics from scratch using the information in this section.

There are four separate acrylic sheets, two for the GPS panel and two for the Autopilot panel. Each sheet is a 150mm x 280mm rectangle cut from 2mm acrylic. Circular holes are drilled to mount the components.

You will find below illustrations and precise numeric specifications for positioning the holes in each case. The best way to use this information is to create a full-scale guide graphic that you can mount temporarily between the two acrylics for the panel you are working on. This will provide you a drilling template with visible centre marks for each hole. You can then use the guide graphic as the basis for creating your final graphic, which ensure that the labels and other graphics will match the locations of your holes precisely.

Alternatively, you can use the numeric information provided to measure directly onto the surface of the acrylic sheets and mark the centre points with a marker pen. This will permit more precise drilling as there will be no parallax error when lining up the drill (if you are working to the guide graphic your drill will be 2mm above the printed mark). A combination of both of these methods will give the best results.

As people will be using different graphics editing software I will not give detailed information about how to do things. You will be best served by using a package that can use layers, such as Photoshop. Many other graphics editors can read and write

Photoshop .PSD files, which preserve the layer information. To create the graphics in a usable format you have two options:

(1) Take a snapshot of the illustration and scale it up to the correct size in your graphic editor. You can easily do this if you are reading this book on the free Kindle for PC application. I use the Snipping tool that comes with Windows 7 to capture the snapshot. You will need to make a judgement of how precisely this allows you to locate the holes.

(2) Using the illustration as a guide, create a new file from scratch in your chosen graphic editor and position the holes precisely using the data tables supplied.

I have supplied enough information for you to be able to find a combination of these two steps that works for you. It is crucial that you can print your graphic at the right size, so you need to spend some time familiarising yourself with your graphic editor and its particular printing foibles. Beware of your printer driver settings too – many drivers will have some kind of 'scale to fit' switch selected by default, which will mess things up. You need to guarantee that something specified as, say, 10cm long on screen will actually be 10cm long if you measure it on the printed page with a ruler.

It is worth including a border on your guide graphic so that you can line it up precisely – any skewing of the image at this stage will inevitably mean that the final panel is not straight. You may or may not be able to correct a small error by skewing the final graphic slightly to compensate, but if it is too far out you're going to end up with a wonky panel one way or the other.

The scaled-up illustration captured from here will not be of sufficient quality to create the final graphic but you can use your graphics editor to reconstruct it using the captured image as a guide (this works best if your editor supports layers and transparency). You can, of course, change the details of the captions, fonts and colours but be cautious about changing the text sizes and positions too much. In particular, I have established a practical separation of the captions from the components by experiment so you should think twice about moving the captions closer.

One final hint on preparing the final graphic is to extend it at the margins by a few millimetres. (This is on the presumption that your background is black or coloured.) You will trim the graphic to the exact size of the panels during assembly and this slight over-sizing of the margins ensures your graphic will be big enough to extend slightly beyond the edges of the acrylic panels. If you attempt to print the graphic exactly to size you risk getting a white line at one or more edges. (Note that you are simply extending the margins, not re-sizing the graphic itself.)

GPS panel graphics

The following illustrations show the final graphic, including crosshairs for the hole centres, and the holes drawn to scale and labelled. The positions and sizes of the holes are specified in the tables that follow the illustrations.

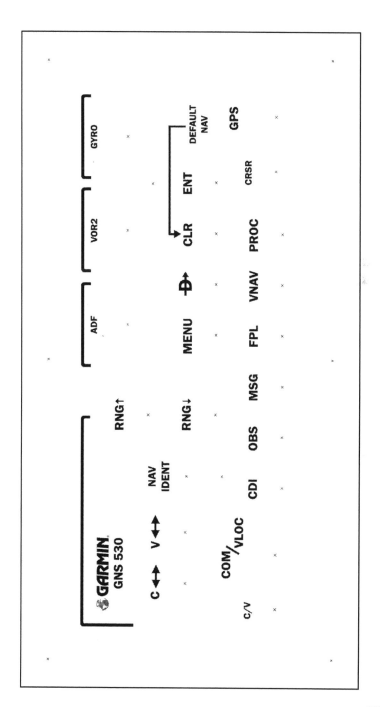

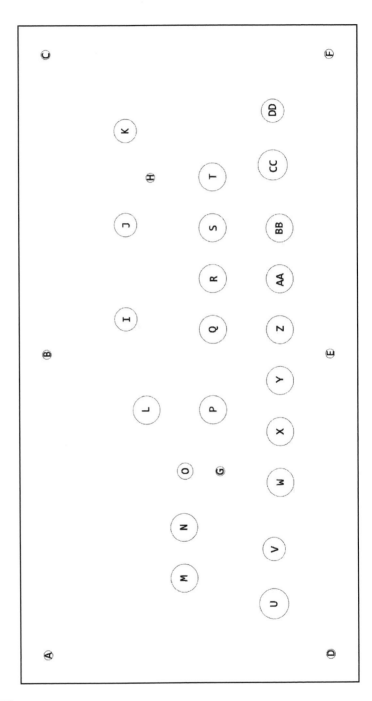

GPS panel front sheet specifications

The table shows the centre (x, y) offset and radius of each hole. The origin (0, 0) is at the (top, left). All dimensions are mm.

hole	x	y	radius
A	12.5	12.5	2
B	140.0	12.5	2
C	267.5	12.5	2
D	12.5	137.5	2
E	140.0	137.5	2
F	267.5	137.5	2
G	90.5	89.0	2
H	215.0	58.5	2
I	155.0	47.5	5
J	195.0	47.5	5
K	235.0	47.5	5
L	116.5	56.5	6
M	45.0	73.0	6
N	66.5	73.0	6
O	90.0	73.0	3.5
P	116.5	86.0	6
Q	150.4	86.0	6
R	172.0	86.0	6
S	193.6	86.0	6
T	215.2	86.0	6
U	34.0	112.5	6.5
V	57.0	112.5	5
W	85.4	115.3	6
X	107.0	115.3	6
Y	128.6	115.3	6
Z	150.2	115.3	6

AA	171.8	115.3	6
BB	193.4	115.3	6
CC	220.2	112.5	6.5
DD	243.3	112.5	5

GPS panel rear sheet specifications

This is identical to the front sheet except that the following six holes are larger.

hole	x	y	radius
A			
B			
C			
D			
E			
F			
G			
H			
I			11
J			11
K			11
L			
M			
N			
O			6.5
P			
Q			
R			
S			
T			
U			
V			11
W			

X
Y
Z
AA
BB
CC
DD   11

Autopilot panel graphics

As before, the illustrations show the final graphic, including
crosshairs for the hole centres, and the holes drawn to scale
and labelled. The positions and sizes of the holes are specified
in the tables that follow the illustrations.

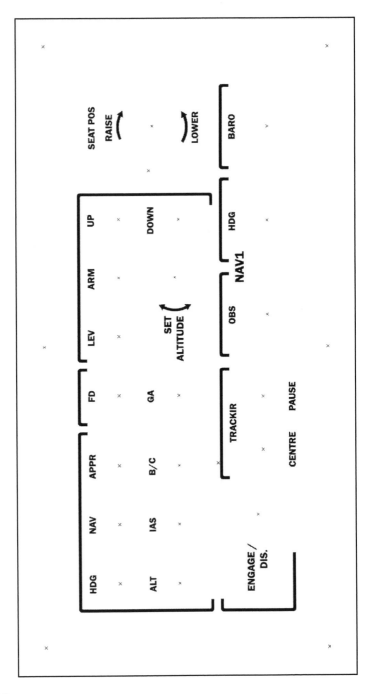

81

Autopilot panel front sheet specifications

The table shows the centre (x, y) offset and radius of each hole. The origin (0, 0) is at the (top, left). All dimensions are mm.

hole	x	y	radius
A	12.5	12.5	2
B	140.0	12.5	2
C	267.5	12.5	2
D	12.5	137.5	2
E	140.0	137.5	2
F	267.5	137.5	2
G	90.5	89.0	2
H	215.0	58.5	2
I	39.5	45.2	6
J	64.5	45.2	6
K	89.5	45.2	6
L	119.3	45.2	6
M	144.4	45.2	6
N	169.4	45.2	6
O	194.4	45.2	6
P	39.5	71.7	6
Q	64.5	71.7	6
R	89.5	71.7	6
S	119.3	71.7	6
T	169.5	70.0	5
U	194.4	71.7	6
V	233.7	60.2	5
W	68.6	106.5	6.5
X	96.3	108.9	6.5
Y	118.8	108.9	6.5
Z	153.8	110.8	5

AA	193.8	110.8	5
BB	233.7	110.8	5

Autopilot panel rear sheet specifications

This is identical to the front sheet except that the following
five holes are larger.

hole	x	y	radius
A			
B			
C			
D			
E			
F			
G			
H			
I			
J			
K			
L			
M			
N			
O			
P			
Q			
R			
S			
T			11
U			
V			11
W			
X			
Y			

Appendix B: Component list

These are the components used in the GPS and Autopilot panels. I have given the brand names and part numbers where possible and linked to the product details at supplier sites where I obtained the parts.

NOTE: the cutout dimensions I have given are the actual dimensions of the cutouts I have used on the acrylic panels, both the hand-made and factory-made variants. These may depart from what the manufacturer specifies but they are the practical dimensions I have established through experimentation.

Leo Bodnar BBI-32 Button Box Interface – with connectors

Rotary Encoder

Cutout: Diameter 10mm, Depth 2mm.
Brand: CTS
Product code: CTS 288V232R161B2
+ knobs (black or grey) for ¼" circular shaft.

Full data sheet:
http://www.ctscorp.com/components/datasheets/288.pdf
(Note that the Bodnar-supplied encoders have imperial specifications. Check the data sheet for specifics of how to decode the part number.)

Square push-buttons (black, red, green)

Cutout: Diameter 12mm, Depth 4mm.
Brand: White Label
Product code: R18-23B-2-H (black)
Product code: R18-23B-6-H (green)

Product code: R18-23B-3-H (red)

Round push-buttons (red, black)

Cutout: Diameter 13mm, depth 4mm.
Product code: R13-510A BLK (red, push-to-make)
Product code: R13-502MC/BLACK (black, changeover)

(NOTE: the black components are changeover switches because this supplier does not appear to stock the simple push-to-make switches in black.)

Miniature latching push switch (red)

Cutout: Diameter 7mm, Depth 2mm.
Brand: SCI
Product code: R13-512B1 RED

Appendix C: Adding a 2D GPS to any add-on aircraft

The default FSX GPS is a 2D gauge that you can install into any aircraft by adding a few lines to the aircraft's panel.cfg file. The simplest way to install it into a new aircraft is to copy it from an existing aircraft. As an example, open up the panel.cfg file for the default Cessna 208B Caravan, which you will find in \fsx\simobjects\airplanes\C208B\panel\panel.cfg.

Near the top of the file you will see a section called [Window Titles], which includes an entry 'Window02=GPS'. A little further down the file you will see a section named 'Window02', which looks like this:

```
[Window02]
Background_color=0,0,0
size_mm=456,378
position=8
visible=0
ident=GPS_PANEL

gauge00=fs9gps!gps_500,  0,0
```

To add the GPS to your own aircraft you can copy this section to the panel.cfg file for your aircraft and then make sure you add a corresponding entry to the [Window Titles] section. The only change you will need to make is to the '02', as each window must have a unique identifier. If 'Window02' is already in use for your aircraft (it probably is), just use the next available unused number. So, for example, if your aircraft already has eleven 2D panels installed (as does the Cessna Caravan), the lines you add to the panel.cfg might look like this:

```
[Window Titles]
```

```
...
Window11=My GPS Panel
...

[Window11]
Background_color=0,0,0
size_mm=456,378
position=8
visible=0
ident=GPS_PANEL

gauge00=fs9gps!gps_500,  0,0
```

The GPS panel can now be selected from the
Views/Instrument Panel menu, where it will have the name
'My GPS Panel'. (For WindowNN numbers below ten these
can also be selected using the shortcut SHIFT+NN.) If you
want to use the portable GPS295 instead of the panel mount
GPS500, just substitute 'gps_295' for 'gps_500' in the last
line. You can also play with the other parameters to change the
initial appearance of the GPS.

Using the GPS on an external monitor

It is possible to use the GPS on a separate monitor, simply by
dragging the 2D panel to it. (If you run in windowed mode you
will need to right-click the panel and select 'undock' first.)
This works fine, although there are a couple of issues to watch
out for. Most importantly, you should NOT try to save a flight
while you have the GPS (or any 2D panel) on the external
monitor. It will not correctly save the position of the 2D panel,
even worse you will lose the panel and not be able to get it
back. You will also discover that the mouse pointer will now
perpetually flash between an arrow and an hourglass and the
only way you can stop it is to restart FSX. If you reload the
saved flight, it happens all over again. Saving flights with 2D
panels off the main screen simply does not work in FSX. You

will find a lot of discussion around this if you Google 'flashing cursor from hell' although it is not, as is often reported, something specific to the Matrox TripleHead2Go.

The other problem with using the 2D GPS on an external screen is more subtle and it is only really a problem if you choose to use a very small screen. Of course this is what many people do and such tiny VGA screens (typically 7" or 10") are widely available for as little as £25, thanks to the boom in reversing cameras and back-seat entertainment systems for cars. The reason this is a problem is that the standard GPS500 and GPS295 gauges do not scale the text and icons according to the size of the GPS window. As the small screen will typically have a high native resolution (1024 x 768 or 800 x 480 are common), this means that the text and icons will be displayed very small and will be barely readable.

You ought to be able to get around this by running your display at a lower resolution if your graphics driver control panel allows this. The actual resolution of a typical GPS display in this class is roughly QVGA (320 x 240 pixels), so if you set your display to run like this you should achieve good results. (You will also typically want to size and position your panel so that the bezels and knobs are clipped off at the sides of the screen, since you will control the GPS with your hardware panel.) The other sure-fire way to get a good readable GPS on a small screen is to purchase the Reality-XP GNS530, which correctly scales the icons and text labels with the size of the panel.

Appendix D: The Almost Aviation Library

An up to date version of this library is available to download from www.almostaviation.com so you should not need to do anything with the text printed here. I have included it because you may be interested in seeing how it works. But if for any reason you cannot download the file you can reconstruct it using the text from here.

```
-- Almost Aviation
-- A few utility functions first

local function nToggleVal(nCurrVal, nVal1, nVal2)
    if nCurrVal == nVal1 then
        return nVal2
    else
        return nVal1
    end
end

local function ShowMessageWindow(Title)
    -- Title, x, y, width and height
    -- (as % of display width and height).
    ipc.setowndisplay(Title, 34.55, 0, 5, 2.5)
end

-- This moves the window off-screen.
local function HideMessageWindow(Title)
    ipc.setowndisplay(Title, 100, 0, 5, 2.5)
end

local function ShowMessage(Message)
    ipc.display(Message)
end

-- Briefly displays a message
local function FlashMessage(Title, Message)
    ShowMessageWindow(Title)
    ShowMessage(Message)
```

```lua
   ipc.sleep(1000)        -- Milliseconds
   HideMessageWindow(Title)
end

-- ## Rotary SHIFT ###############

local RotaryShiftActive = 0
-- Coarse adjustment speed:
local BUG_MULTIPLIER = 10

function AAL_Rotary_Shift_ON()
   RotaryShiftActive = 1
end

function AAL_Rotary_Shift_OFF()
   RotaryShiftActive = 0
end

-- ## Autopilot ###############

local AP_TargetAltitude = 0

function AAL_AP_Master_Toggle()
   if ipc.readUD(0x07BC) == 1 then
      -- Offset from FSUIPC documentation
      _AUTOPILOT_OFF()
   else
      _AUTOPILOT_ON()
      _AP_WING_LEVELER_ON()
   end
end

function AAL_AP_Master_ON()
   _AUTOPILOT_ON()
   _AP_WING_LEVELER_ON()
end

function AAL_AP_Master_OFF()
   _AUTOPILOT_OFF()
end

function AAL_AP_FD_Flight_Director()
   _TOGGLE_FLIGHT_DIRECTOR()
end
```

```lua
function AAL_AP_HDG_Heading_Hold()
   _AP_PANEL_HEADING_HOLD()
end

function AAL_AP_IAS_Airspeed_Hold()
   _AP_PANEL_SPEED_HOLD()
end

function AAL_AP_NAV_NAV1_Hold()
   _AP_NAV1_HOLD()
end

function AAL_AP_APR_Approach_Hold()
   _AP_APR_HOLD()
end

function AAL_AP_REV_Back_Course_Hold()
   _AP_BC_HOLD()
end

function AAL_AP_GA_Go_Around()
   _AUTO_THROTTLE_TO_GA()
end

local function QueryAltHold()
   return ipc.readUD(0x07D0)
end

local function GetCurrentAlt()
   return ipc.readSD(0x3324)
end

local function QueryUnitsFeet()
   return ipc.readUW(0x0C18) ~= 2
   -- 0 = US, 1 =hybrid, 2 = metric
end

local function EngageAltHold(TargetAlt)
   if QueryUnitsFeet() then
      _AP_ALT_VAR_SET_ENGLISH(TargetAlt)
   else
      _AP_ALT_VAR_SET_METRIC(TargetAlt)
   end
```

```
      _AP_ALT_HOLD_ON()
end

function AAL_AP_ALT_Hold_Current_Altitude()
   _AP_ALT_HOLD()
end

function AAL_AP_Decrease_Target_Altitude()
   _AP_ALT_HOLD_OFF()

   local nSteps = 1

   if RotaryShiftActive == 1 then
      nSteps = BUG_MULTIPLIER
   end

   for n = 1, nSteps do
      _AP_ALT_VAR_DEC()
   end
end

function AAL_AP_Increase_Target_Altitude()
   _AP_ALT_HOLD_OFF()

   local nSteps = 1

   if RotaryShiftActive == 1 then
      nSteps = BUG_MULTIPLIER
   end

   for n = 1, nSteps do
      _AP_ALT_VAR_INC()
   end
end

function AAL_AP_ARM_Hold_Target_Altitude()
   if QueryAltHold() == 1 then
      _AP_ALT_HOLD_OFF()
   Else
      -- The target altitude is in metres,
      -- so we must convert
      EngageAltHold(3.25 *
                ipc.readUD(0x07D4) / 65536)
   end
```

```
end

function AAL_AP_LEV_Wing_Leveler()
   _AP_WING_LEVELER()
end

function AAL_AP_UP_Increase_Vertical_Speed()
   _AP_VS_VAR_INC()
end

function AAL_AP_DN_Decrease_Vertical_Speed()
   _AP_VS_VAR_DEC()
end

function AAL_AP_UP_Attitude_Hold_Increase_Pitch()
   _AP_ATT_HOLD_ON()
   _AP_PITCH_REF_INC_UP()
   _AP_ALT_HOLD_OFF()
end

function AAL_AP_DN_Attitude_Hold_Decrease_Pitch()
   _AP_ATT_HOLD_ON()
   _AP_PITCH_REF_INC_DN()
   _AP_ALT_HOLD_OFF()
end

-- ## GPS500 ##############

function AAL_GPS_Toggle_2D()
   _PANEL_ID_TOGGLE(34567)
end

function AAL_GPS_Close_2D()
   _PANEL_ID_CLOSE(34567)
end

function AAL_GPS_Single_GPS_Knob_Left()
   if RotaryShiftActive == 1 then
      AAL_GPS_Outer_Knob_Left()
   else
      AAL_GPS_Inner_Knob_Left()
   end
end
```

```
function AAL_GPS_Single_GPS_Knob_Right()
   if RotaryShiftActive == 1 then
      AAL_GPS_Outer_Knob_Right()
   else
      AAL_GPS_Inner_Knob_Right()
   end
end

function AAL_GPS_Push_Cursor()
   _GPS_CURSOR_BUTTON()
end

function AAL_GPS_Increase_Range()
   _GPS_ZOOMOUT_BUTTON()
end

function AAL_GPS_Decrease_Range()
   _GPS_ZOOMIN_BUTTON()
end

function AAL_GPS_Direct_To()
   _GPS_DIRECTTO_BUTTON()
end

function AAL_GPS_MENU()
   _GPS_MENU_BUTTON()
end

function AAL_GPS_CLR()
   _GPS_CLEAR_BUTTON()
end

function AAL_GPS_ENT()
   _GPS_ENTER_BUTTON()
end

function AAL_GPS_CDI()
   _TOGGLE_GPS_DRIVES_NAV1()
end

function AAL_GPS_OBS()
   _GPS_OBS_BUTTON()
end
```

```
function AAL_GPS_MSG()
   _GPS_MSG_BUTTON()
end

function AAL_GPS_FPL()
   _GPS_FLIGHTPLAN_BUTTON()
end

function AAL_GPS_VNAV()
   _GPS_TERRAIN_BUTTON()
end

function AAL_GPS_PROC()
   _GPS_PROCEDURE_BUTTON()
end

function AAL_GPS_Nearest()
   _GPS_NEAREST_BUTTON()
end


-- We can use the left knob to control the radios
-- just like the GNS530. This is the same as the
-- fake GNS530 in the Aerosoft Twin Otter. The
-- Twin Otter keeps track internally of which
-- radio we're addressing, but we have do it
-- manually with our own local variable.

local ComNavSelect = 0  -- 0 if COM1 radio is
   selected, 1 if NAV1 is selected

function AAL_GPS_COM_NAV_Swap()
    ComNavSelect = nToggleVal(ComNavSelect, 0, 1)
end

-- This is the same as the above function but
-- briefly displays a message showing which radio
-- is now active.
function AAL_GPS_COM_NAV_Swap_With_Display()
   ComNavSelect = nToggleVal(ComNavSelect, 0, 1)
   local Message
   if ComNavSelect == 0 then
      Message = "COM1 radio"
   else
      Message = "NAV1 radio"
```

```
      end

   FlashMessage("Adjusting", Message)
end

function AAL_GPS_Single_Radio_Knob_Left()
   if RotaryShiftActive == 1 then
      AAL_Radio_Outer_Knob_Left()
   else
      AAL_Radio_Inner_Knob_Left()
   end
end

function AAL_GPS_Single_Radio_Knob_Right()
   if RotaryShiftActive == 1 then
      AAL_Radio_Outer_Knob_Right()
   else
      AAL_Radio_Inner_Knob_Right()
   end
end

function AAL_GPS_NAV1_Ident_ON()
   _RADIO_VOR1_IDENT_ENABLE()
end

function AAL_GPS_NAV1_Ident_OFF()
   _RADIO_VOR1_IDENT_DISABLE()
end

function AAL_GPS_NAV1_Ident_TOGGLE()
   _RADIO_VOR1_IDENT_TOGGLE()
end

function AAL_GPS_COM1_Swap_Freq()
   _COM_STBY_RADIO_SWAP()
end

function AAL_GPS_NAV1_Swap_Freq()
   _NAV1_RADIO_SWAP()
end

-- ## Extra Rotary Knobs ##############

function AAL_ADF_Card_Left()
```

```
    local nSteps = 1

    if RotaryShiftActive == 1 then
       nSteps = BUG_MULTIPLIER
    end

    for n = 1, nSteps do
       _ADF_CARD_DEC()
    end
end

function AAL_ADF_Card_Right()
    local nSteps = 1

    if RotaryShiftActive == 1 then
       nSteps = BUG_MULTIPLIER
    end

    for n = 1, nSteps do
       _ADF_CARD_INC()
    end
end

function AAL_VOR1_OBS_Left()
    local nSteps = 1

    if RotaryShiftActive == 1 then
       nSteps = BUG_MULTIPLIER
    end

    for n = 1, nSteps do
       _VOR1_OBI_DEC()
    end
end

function AAL_VOR1_OBS_Right()
    local nSteps = 1

    if RotaryShiftActive == 1 then
       nSteps = BUG_MULTIPLIER
    end

    for n = 1, nSteps do
       _VOR1_OBI_INC()
```

```
   end
end

function AAL_VOR2_OBS_Left()
   local nSteps = 1

   if RotaryShiftActive == 1 then
      nSteps = BUG_MULTIPLIER
   end

   for n = 1, nSteps do
      _VOR2_OBI_DEC()
   end
end

function AAL_VOR2_OBS_Right()
   local nSteps = 1

   if RotaryShiftActive == 1 then
      nSteps = BUG_MULTIPLIER
   end

   for n = 1, nSteps do
      _VOR2_OBI_INC()
   end
end

function AAL_Heading_Bug_Left()
   local nSteps = 1

   if RotaryShiftActive == 1 then
      nSteps = BUG_MULTIPLIER
   end

   for n = 1, nSteps do
      _HEADING_BUG_DEC()
   end
end

function AAL_Heading_Bug_Right()
   local nSteps = 1

   if RotaryShiftActive == 1 then
      nSteps = BUG_MULTIPLIER
```

```
      end

      for n = 1, nSteps do
         _HEADING_BUG_INC()
      end
end

function AAL_Altimeter_Left()
   local nSteps = 1

   if RotaryShiftActive == 1 then
      nSteps = BUG_MULTIPLIER
   end

   for n = 1, nSteps do
      _KOHLSMAN_DEC()
   end
end

function AAL_Altimeter_Right()
   local nSteps = 1

   if RotaryShiftActive == 1 then
      nSteps = BUG_MULTIPLIER
   end

   for n = 1, nSteps do
      _KOHLSMAN_INC()
   end
end

function AAL_Gyro_Left()
   local nSteps = 1

   if RotaryShiftActive == 1 then
      nSteps = BUG_MULTIPLIER
   end

   for n = 1, nSteps do
      _GYRO_DRIFT_DEC()
   end
end

function AAL_Gyro_Right()
```

```lua
    local nSteps = 1

    if RotaryShiftActive == 1 then
        nSteps = BUG_MULTIPLIER
    end

    for n = 1, nSteps do
        _GYRO_DRIFT_INC()
    end
end

-- ## Eyepoint ###############

-- Some of the functions below generate keystrokes
-- that are aimed at a particular application -
-- either TrackIR or EZCA. The keystrokes are
-- hard-coded here and are chosen simply because
-- these are what I currently have set. If your
-- keystrokes are different you will need to
-- either (a) change them to match what I generate
-- here, or (b) change these functions to generate
-- the keystrokes you have set. You can find the
-- information for generating keystrokes in lib-
-- realityxp.lua.
--
-- It is also important to ensure you do not use
-- the same keystrokes for different functions in
-- other applications. For example, it is easy to
-- discover that a keystroke you are using the
-- toggle the TrackIR on and off is also changing
-- the elevator trim or something similar.
-- Remember that even if you have 'use
-- controllers' selected OFF in FSX, keystroke
-- bindings are still active.

-- Keystrokes intercepted by TrackIR

function AAL_TrackIR_Toggle()
    -- CTRL + SHIFT + Q
    ipc.keypress(81, 11)
end

function AAL_TrackIR_Centre()
    -- CTRL + SHIFT + K
```

```
      ipc.keypress(75, 11)
end

-- Commands directly to FSX

local function Eyepoint_Up()
   _EYEPOINT_UP()
end

local function Eyepoint_Down()
   _EYEPOINT_DOWN()
end

local function Eyepoint_Left()
   _EYEPOINT_LEFT()
end

local function Eyepoint_Right()
   _EYEPOINT_RIGHT()
end

local function Eyepoint_Back()
   _EYEPOINT_BACK()
end

local function Eyepoint_Forward()
   _EYEPOINT_FORWARD()
end

local EYEPOINT_SPEED = 10

function AAL_Eyepoint_Up()
   local nSteps = 1

   if RotaryShiftActive == 0 then
      nSteps = EYEPOINT_SPEED
   end

   for n = 1, nSteps do
      Eyepoint_Up()
   end
end

function AAL_Eyepoint_Down()
```

102

```
   local nSteps = 1

   if RotaryShiftActive == 0 then
      nSteps = EYEPOINT_SPEED
   end

   for n = 1, nSteps do
      Eyepoint_Down()
   end
end

function AAL_Eyepoint_Up_Or_Forward()
   if RotaryShiftActive == 1 then
      Eyepoint_Forward()
   else
      Eyepoint_Up()
   end
end

function AAL_Eyepoint_Down_Or_Back()
   if RotaryShiftActive == 1 then
      Eyepoint_Back()
   else
      Eyepoint_Down()
   end
end

function AAL_Eyepoint_Up_Or_Right()
   if RotaryShiftActive == 1 then
      Eyepoint_Right()
   else
      Eyepoint_Up()
   end
end

function AAL_Eyepoint_Down_Or_Left()
   if RotaryShiftActive == 1 then
      Eyepoint_Left()
   else
      Eyepoint_Down()
   end
end

function AAL_Eyepoint_Reset()
```

```
      _EYEPOINT_RESET()
end

-- Keystrokes intercepted by EZCA

local function EZCA_Eyepoint_Up()
   -- CTRL + RIGHT
   ipc.keypress(39, 10)
end

local function EZCA_Eyepoint_Down()
   -- CTRL + LEFT
   ipc.keypress(37, 10)
end

local function EZCA_Eyepoint_Left()
   -- CTRL + PgUP
   ipc.keypress(33, 10)
end

local function EZCA_Eyepoint_Right()
   -- CTRL + PgDN
   ipc.keypress(34, 10)
end

local function EZCA_Eyepoint_Back()
   -- CTRL + Down Arrow
   ipc.keypress(40, 10)
end

local function EZCA_Eyepoint_Forward()
   -- CTRL + Up Arrow
   ipc.keypress(38, 10)
end

function AAL_EZCA_Eyepoint_Up_Or_Forward()
   if RotaryShiftActive == 1 then
      EZCA_Eyepoint_Forward()
   else
      EZCA_Eyepoint_Up()
   end
end

function AAL_EZCA_Eyepoint_Down_Or_Back()
```

104

```
   if RotaryShiftActive == 1 then
      EZCA_Eyepoint_Back()
   else
      EZCA_Eyepoint_Down()
   end
end

function AAL_EZCA_Eyepoint_Up_Or_Right()
   if RotaryShiftActive == 1 then
      EZCA_Eyepoint_Right()
   else
      EZCA_Eyepoint_Up()
   end
end

function AAL_EZCA_Eyepoint_Down_Or_Left()
   if RotaryShiftActive == 1 then
      EZCA_Eyepoint_Left()
   else
      EZCA_Eyepoint_Down()
   end
end

-- ## GPS500 (dual concentric functions) ######

function AAL_Radio_Outer_Knob_Left()
   if ComNavSelect == 0 then
      _COM_RADIO_WHOLE_DEC()
   else
      _NAV1_RADIO_WHOLE_DEC()
   end
end

function AAL_Radio_Outer_Knob_Right()
   if ComNavSelect == 0 then
      _COM_RADIO_WHOLE_INC()
   else
      _NAV1_RADIO_WHOLE_INC()
   end
end

function AAL_Radio_Inner_Knob_Left()
   if ComNavSelect == 0 then
      _COM_RADIO_FRACT_DEC()
```

```
      else
         _NAV1_RADIO_FRACT_DEC()
      end
end

function AAL_Radio_Inner_Knob_Right()
   if ComNavSelect == 0 then
      _COM_RADIO_FRACT_INC()
   else
      _NAV1_RADIO_FRACT_INC()
   end
end

function AAL_GPS_Outer_Knob_Left()
   _GPS_GROUP_KNOB_DEC()
end

function AAL_GPS_Outer_Knob_Right()
   _GPS_GROUP_KNOB_INC()
end

function AAL_GPS_Inner_Knob_Left()
   _GPS_PAGE_KNOB_DEC()
end

function AAL_GPS_Inner_Knob_Right()
   _GPS_PAGE_KNOB_INC()
end

-- ## GNS530 (Aerosoft single rotary funcs) #####

-- For the full implementation of the GNS530 you
-- will also need the Twin Otter Extended LINDA
-- library, available free from the LINDA
-- downloads forum. The following functions are
-- just to add the single-rotary support.

local function GNS530_GPS_Outer_Knob_Left()
   _GPS_GROUP_KNOB_DEC()
end

local function GNS530_GPS_Outer_Knob_Right()
   _GPS_GROUP_KNOB_INC()
end
```

```
local function GNS530_GPS_Inner_Knob_Left()
   _GPS_PAGE_KNOB_DEC()
end

local function GNS530_GPS_Inner_Knob_Right()
   _GPS_PAGE_KNOB_INC()
end

function AAL_AS_GNS530_Single_GPS_Knob_Left()
   if RotaryShiftActive == 1 then
      GNS530_GPS_Outer_Knob_Left()
   else
      GNS530_GPS_Inner_Knob_Left()
   end
end

function AAL_AS_GNS530_Single_GPS_Knob_Right()
   if RotaryShiftActive == 1 then
      GNS530_GPS_Outer_Knob_Right()
   else
      GNS530_GPS_Inner_Knob_Right()
   end
end

local function GNS530_Radio_Outer_Knob_Left()
   if ipc.ReadLvar("L:GPS_ComNav_select") == 0
   then
      _COM_RADIO_WHOLE_DEC()
   else
      _NAV1_RADIO_WHOLE_DEC()
   end
end

local function GNS530_Radio_Outer_Knob_Right()
   if ipc.ReadLvar("L:GPS_ComNav_select") == 0
   then
      _COM_RADIO_WHOLE_INC()
   else
      _NAV1_RADIO_WHOLE_INC()
   end
end

local function GNS530_Radio_Inner_Knob_Left()
```

```lua
      if ipc.ReadLvar("L:GPS_ComNav_select") == 0
      then
         _COM_RADIO_FRACT_DEC()
      else
         _NAV1_RADIO_FRACT_DEC()
      end
end

local function GNS530_Radio_Inner_Knob_Right()
   if ipc.ReadLvar("L:GPS_ComNav_select") == 0
   then
      _COM_RADIO_FRACT_INC()
   else
      _NAV1_RADIO_FRACT_INC()
   end
end

function AAL_AS_GNS530_Single_Radio_Knob_Left()
   if RotaryShiftActive == 1 then
      GNS530_Radio_Outer_Knob_Left()
   else
      GNS530_Radio_Inner_Knob_Left()
   end
end

function AAL_AS_GNS530_Single_Radio_Knob_Right()
   if RotaryShiftActive == 1 then
      AAL_AS_GNS530_Radio_Outer_Knob_Right()
   else
      AAL_AS_GNS530_Radio_Inner_Knob_Right()
   end
end

-- ## GNS530 (Reality XP single rotary funcs) ###

-- We can just use the RXP library functions
-- directly except for the single-knob rotary
-- encoders, which we need to manage using
-- the SHIFT function.

function AAL_RXP530_Single_GPS_Knob_Left()
   if RotaryShiftActive == 1 then
      RXP_530_RKNOBO_L()
   else
```

```
            RXP_530_RKNOBI_L()
    end
end

function AAL_RXP530_Single_GPS_Knob_Right()
    if RotaryShiftActive == 1 then
        RXP_530_RKNOBO_R()
    else
        RXP_530_RKNOBI_R()
    end
end

function AAL_RXP530_Single_Radio_Knob_Left()
    if RotaryShiftActive == 1 then
        RXP_530_LKNOBO_L()
    else
        RXP_530_LKNOBI_L()
    end
end

function AAL_RXP530_Single_Radio_Knob_Right()
    if RotaryShiftActive == 1 then
        RXP_530_LKNOBO_R()
    else
        RXP_530_LKNOBI_R()
    end
end

_log("Almost Aviation library loaded...")
```

Made in the USA
Middletown, DE
16 February 2019